About the Author

J.C. AMBERCHELE was born in Philadelphia in 1940, attended a Quaker school, then college in Pennsylvania and New York, earning a B.A. in psychology. He first became interested in the nature of the Self in the 1960s when he took LSD, but didn't become deeply involved in spiritual matters until after he went to prison and tried meditation in the 1980s. During that time, he studied the works of Wei Wu Wei, Ramana Maharshi, Nisargadatta Maharaj and many others, until happening upon an article by Douglas Harding that allowed him to actually see Who he really is. Since then, he has been practicing Seeing, and is the author of two previous books on the subject: *The Light That I Am: Notes From The Ground of Being;* and *The Almighty Mackerel and His Holy Bootstraps: Waking Up to Who You Really Are*, both published by Non-Duality Press. He has been incarcerated for more than 30 years, and does not expect to be released soon.

Also by J.C. Amberchele and published
by Non-Duality Press ✎

The Light That I Am
The Almighty Mackerel and His Holy Bootstraps

THE HEAVENLY BACKFLIP:

Seeing And Being The Unfigureoutable

By J.C. Amberchele

NON-DUALITY PRESS

THE HEAVENLY BACKFLIP

First edition published September 2012 by NON-DUALITY PRESS

© J.C. Amberchele 2012
© Non-Duality Press 2012

NON-DUALITY PRESS | PO Box 2228 | Salisbury | SP2 2GZ
United Kingdom

ISBN: 978-1-908664-23-5

www.non-dualitypress.org

TABLE OF CONTENTS

LOOK!

Sometimes I want to stop
the first person I see and shout,
LOOK! LOOK! Isn't this
MIRACULOUS?

But of course they'd think I was crazy
and step around me and hurry
on their way.

But no matter, no matter, I say,
for you see, I've
HAPPENED!

Isn't that MARVELOUS?
Like Jack sprung from an invisible box,
I've popped up out of
NOWHERE!

Literally nowhere,
and with no help, and for no reason
but to
BE!

So come. Come from
your contraction, confrontation, insanity.
See how you
VANISH!

And find in your place this wild spectacle,
this riot of sound and shape and color, this
wondrous world that is your Self!

All

right

Here!

INTRODUCTION

WHAT AM I?

The Great Ones, the sages of every age, tell me what to look for. They say that the answer lies not elsewhere but right where I am, here where I am both the center and the source of the universe. They say that, contrary to what I may *think* I am, what I really am is formless, boundless, timeless, and deathless; that I am utterly transparent, empty, not an object. They say that this clarity that lies at the very heart of my humanity is none other than the Self, God, Buddha, Tao, and the Beloved, and that to see and be this requires no change, no achievement, no struggle, for it is already what I am; in fact, I cannot *not* be it. They say that no one else can tell me what I am, that I must see for myself, and should I discover this and live consciously from this, all will be right, all will be true.

This one story, the story of One, has been called the Perennial Philosophy, and is said to be the root message of all the major religions, a message long ago buried in the pronouncements of those who did not understand. But now it is widely available again, this time as the message of Non-duality, in books and at gatherings and online. The WORD—simple, precise, direct—is alive and well and making the rounds, for all who are ready to hear.

And even more direct—that is, direct to this core of Luminous Awareness—is the VISION, the *seeing* of what you are, where you are. This vision is so simple, so easy to see, it is mostly overlooked. And for good reason—*it is what is looking.* And it is this "looking at what is looking," actually looking back at what you are looking out of, that is the theme of this book.

According to the *Tao Te Ching*, the Tao that can be spoken is not the Tao. One can only point in the direction of awakening, and while most of the pointers in the Non-duality message are conceptual, there is one pointer that dispenses with words and actually, physically points at the Luminous Awareness that you are. It is your index finger, pointing at where you thought you had a face, the same face that others see and say you have, but where you see only emptiness, no-thing, that which was once referred to as your "Original Face," the one you had before you were born and the one only you can see, right where you are. It is the face of First-Person-Singular, Present Tense, also called the Self, God, Buddha, and the Beloved. It is what you really are and always have been: formless, boundless, timeless, somehow awake, somehow knowing, forever unknown.

The writings and dialogues in this book are offered, then, as pointers, arrows aimed at Who You Really Are. May you see and be what you already are. May you see and be THIS: undeniable, unfigureoutable.

BACKFLIP

Jump back. Do a backflip into Who You Are. It's not there, it's here. All of it. It's all internal. There's no outside. There's no inside, even. It all just IS, for no reason other than heaven. Who are we and what are we doing? This is it! Simply THIS. We're worlding. We're universing. And we're not "we." We're I, awake to the fact of Awakeness, aware, unborn, knowing.

Jump back.

ENLIGHTENMENT

What's your take on enlightenment? I've read about all the great spiritual masters who were enlightened, about the Buddha being enlightened.

No one has ever been enlightened.

So what does enlightenment mean, then?

The best definition I've heard is that enlightenment is the absence of anyone to be enlightened. Put it this way, it's not something you "get." It's not attained because it's what you already are, and what you already are is the absence of what you think you are, a separate, self-existing "self." It's also a term that people use to distinguish between those who supposedly know how things really are and those who don't, the "enlightened" and the "endarkened," which makes no sense to those who know how things really are.

Then why do people strive for it?

Because it's the best game in town, especially when other games are seen through and no longer work. One gets to be "spiritual," a seeker of truth. One has apparent meaning in their life, and can join others who have similar aspirations. One gets to be pious, righteous, and may even experience spiritual "highs" from time to time.

What's so bad about that?

Nothing. It's not bad, it's just not different from any other game of being "somebody" and having a "life." It's no different from being a doctor, a janitor, or a car mechanic.

People want to get free, and think enlightenment is freedom. Apparently you disagree.

They were never bound, and in seeking enlightenment, they bind themselves all the more. It's the same with "awakening"—they were never asleep, and only sink deeper into dreamland by trying to wake up.

So what can be done? How does anyone go about waking up?

They don't. What we're talking about here is merely a shift in perception, and no one does it. It just happens. I can tell you to try this method or that, but it won't make a bit of difference unless you're ready, and I don't even know what "ready" means.

So you're not enlightened?

No.

Then why are we having this conversation?

Because you think I can help you find enlightenment?

Yes, I guess that's the reason.

Well, sorry to disappoint you, but in the end, others can't help you. At some point The Absolute—Who You Really Are—chooses to consciously know itself, and in a flash of *insight*, turns in on itself, *sees* itself, looks back on itself and recognizes the Empty Awareness that it is. It's called Seeing, and it doesn't happen to a separate self for the obvious reason that the separate self is an object, an appearance *in*

Seeing, *in* Who You Really Are, and can therefore never see, never know, anything.

This Seeing can be the end of the road, the end of seeking. Or it can be the beginning of a process of confirmation whereby years are spent meditating, reading, meeting with others interested in spiritual matters, and maybe inquiring into the nature of the separate self, searching it out, pinning it down, discovering where it resides if it resides anywhere. This inquiry may reveal the real story of the separate self, that one's identity as the body and mind is in fact just that—a story. In this way, perhaps over and over, as the mind repeatedly searches for and repeatedly fails to find a separate self, conditioning is eroded, and one's identity is left suspended in the unknown.

What happens then? Will I be lost, or will I be awake?

Who you think you are will perhaps be lost, but never awake. Who You Really Are is Awakeness Itself, and can never be lost.

Well, I feel a little lost right now.

Hang in there, it only gets worse—and that's the good news!

LOOK AT WHAT YOU ARE LOOKING OUT OF

LOOK AT WHAT YOU ARE LOOKING OUT OF, and notice that there are...

NO BOUNDARIES—Like an open window with no frame, lit from within, notice how huge it is, that the whole world easily fits inside it, for it is entirely...

EMPTY—Not a speck of anything gets in the way. And because it is entirely empty, it is...

ENTIRELY FILLED—With the scene. And it isn't just "space" for the scene, it *is* the scene! Thus, it is WHAT IS. And all of it is presented right...

HERE—And it is wide, wide...

AWAKE!

THIS IS WHAT YOU ARE!

(Search the universe far and wide, and you will never find another awareness. There is only THIS, and it is boundless, empty, filled with the scene, right here, and awake. It is Who You Are, and you are THE ALONE.)

JOURNEY TO HERE

I read something today in a book by a Buddhist nun that was discouraging. She was saying that this is as good as it gets, that the journey of self-improvement—bettering oneself, becoming wiser and more peaceful over the years—is an illusion. This goes against the grain of everything I've been taught. It goes against the grain of the society we live in. And one of the reasons I came to Buddhism in the first place was because I felt it would make me a better person.

"This is as good as it gets." Who better to have uttered that great line than Jack Nicholson?

Oh… yeah… you're talking about the film.

Yes. But it also could have been uttered by the Buddha. There is not, never was, and never will be a journey. Not of self-improvement, not of life, not even from point A to point B! There is only THIS, appearing as a journey: THIS, pretending to go out and return to Itself, but never being other than Itself.

But don't you find that depressing? Without a journey, without goals and achievement, what's the use of living? Life would be so boring and meaningless.

On the contrary, what a relief! There's no pressure to perform. There's no search. There's nothing to be other than what you are. And instead of the boring daily struggle of hauling an illusory self up an illusory mountain of personal improvement, all the while missing the fabulous view, there is the excitement of not only *what* shows up but *that* it shows up, right now. What could be more meaningful or less dreary?

So it's like I need to walk instead of run—is that what you're saying? I need to slow down and notice my surroundings more?

No, there's nothing you need to do. What I'm saying points to a fundamental change of outlook, the difference between seeing from the point of view of, as you said, "everything you've been taught," to seeing reality exactly as it is, without the filter of believing you are a separate self. Buddhism isn't about making you a better person. Buddhism is about discovering you are much more and much less than a person. When that is realized, the entire structure of a life involving a past and a future changes. This fundamental change has been called *metanoesis,* or *paravritti*—turning away from the mistaken belief that you're a separate self up against a hostile world "out there." It's the holy backflip, and it's not about a "you" doing anything, improving or not improving.

But what about the Buddhist doctrine of accumulating merit, so that one can be reborn into a more favorable life next time around?

Well, let's just say that Buddhism, like all the other major religions, has its share of foolishness. I can't imagine the Buddha having said one word about accumulating merit, and if he did, surely it was taken out of context or misquoted or in some way reworded years later by those who didn't understand. A doctrine such as that only perpetuates the false belief of being a separate self, the very belief that Buddhism intends to dispel.

So would you say it's a matter of not knowing where you're going?

Well...

Because at least I wouldn't be on a journey, setting goals, trying to have a better life.

Yes, as long as you don't set the goal of not setting goals, you might at least relax. And just maybe the idea that you are merely a separate self will relax also. Try to relax, however, and you'll continue perpetuating that self. This is difficult to hear, I know. It's very deflating to learn that you can't do anything about anything. The good news is that it happens, and when it does, the response can be laughter, awe, relief, and gratitude. However, even what is said here is misleading because it's not an event in the usual sense of the word. It happens outside the concept of time. But it's known, because it's your essence, your nature, as What Is.

Well, how can I know it?

You can't know it because it's not an object. It itself is the knowing. "Hows" and "whys" have no relevance. There's no answer to "how" because it can only lead away from where you are, and there's no answer to "why" because, since there's nothing other than THIS, there's no causal relationship to something else. This is it! This is as good as it gets, and it's What you Are.

QUANDARY

How to say it? How to describe what this is?

I might say what I am not, but even *that* is what I am, for there is nothing apart from what I am. I am Pure Awareness manifesting as this and that, and this and that are what I am: Pure Awareness.

The Negative Way—*neti neti*, "not this, not that"—taken to the limit, might reveal what I am, but only because, taken to the limit, all that is negated is then seen to be what I am!

I am Awareness filled with everything, and not as two. I am void/form. I am Pure Subjectivity. I am Awakeness, Presence, Being… and none of these.

This much I know: I am a quandary unto myself.

SO WHAT?

The way I see it, there are levels of consciousness, and right now we are at an evolutionary stage where more and more people are approaching enlightenment because they are functioning from a higher plane, so to speak.

How do you figure?

In the past, there were a few people here and there who were enlightened, like the Buddha and a couple of his followers, some Zen Masters in China and Japan, a scattering of holy men in India—but now with the internet and globalization, thousands of people are waking up all over the world. Along with this, man is evolving psychically, expanding his consciousness, maybe even developing a larger brain. There are the old stories of how enlightened beings could levitate or fly or be in two places at once, or even walk through walls. I think we'll see more of that in the near future because we'll be operating from a higher level of consciousness.

How could anyone approach enlightenment when what they already are is enlightenment itself? How could there be an enlightened being when enlightenment means that there is no separate being to be it? How could consciousness come in levels when all levels are in consciousness? How can you be in two places at once when you're nowhere at all?

I take it you don't agree.

No, I don't. All that mumbo jumbo about "levels of consciousness" and "approaching enlightenment" only functions to keep you trapped in the notion of being a separate self in a world of separate things. The same for the *siddhis*—the magical powers that one hopes to gain or attain to when "enlightened." You can walk through walls? So what? You can levitate or fly around the block? Big deal. None of it means anything to Who You Really Are; none is a pre-requisite for becoming Who You Really Are nor a result of discovering Who You Really Are. You are That right now.

Yeah, but that's so deflating. It means I'm stuck with the way things are right now, and I don't particularly like the way things are. It feels like giving up. Plus, I can't believe that any old Joe Schmo could be enlightened.

You're not stuck with the way things are. The way things are is What You Are! You've got one thing right, though—any old Joe Schmo can't be enlightened. No one can.

But it can't just be what's going on right now.

Again, coming from your notion of being a separate self, it isn't what you think is going on. As Who You Really Are, it is *exactly* what is going on. In fact, Who You Really Are *is* what is going on, including, even, your notion of being a separate self.

That's hard to accept. I'm not willing to be the world's punching bag.

No, of course not. If you believe you are self-existing and apart from Oneness, you might win a few rounds, but you'll lose most, and eventually you'll get knocked out of the ring altogether. And that's okay. It's how Who You Really Are is manifesting right now. Right now it's playing the part of a separate individual who doesn't want to be a punching bag but, because of his conditioned beliefs, is bound to be one anyway. If you get around to investigating those beliefs, you may find them to be untrue. Or you could look within—actually take a look at what you are looking out of—and realize Who You Really Are in a flash. By that I mean that you can turn your attention around 180 degrees and see That Which Is Seeing. When I do this, I see nothing. But it's not the kind of nothing that's the opposite of something; it's not a mere blank. This nothing is *aware*. And it's huge, in that everything easily fits within it, including the universe as a whole. Take a look, and take what you see on present evidence, not what you assume or believe because it's what you learned as a child from others. Others (and cameras), from where they are, see a right-side-up human being with a head on top and feet below. But is that what you see from where you are? Are you not, from your point of view, upside-down and headless? Look back. Do you see your face or do you see clear, open, boundless awareness, filled with the scene? Hasn't it always been this way, even though you haven't noticed it? See as a little child would, with that same innocent curiosity prior to thoughts and beliefs. Are you really the way others see and say you are? Why take their word for it, when you can plainly see what you are for yourself?

I don't see the point. That "looking back" thing doesn't do anything for me. I mean, it's interesting and all that, but what's that got to do with enlightenment?

You see, this is what happens when you hold false assumptions and expectations—you want "the point" to be other than what is. Rather than see the truth about Who You Really Are, you seek fireworks and magic. Who You Really Are is all very ordinary, just now, just now, just as it is.

And oh, before I forget, Who You Really Are is the center of the universe, a universe that appears within you, *as* you. So what? Well, some call it God.

SENSATIONAL BODY

Telling the truth, taking exactly what is presented and not what I have learned from others nor what I assume nor imagine, I ask: What is this flesh-body that "follows me around" (as a friend likes to say) all day and night? Is it not, like every other thing, a sensation experienced in and by Awareness? I see it, hear it and feel it as I see, hear and feel other objects, and yet I call this flesh-body "me" and other objects "not me," as though it is the body that experiences the sensations, as though Awareness is a mere by-product of the body, as though what I am *is* the body.

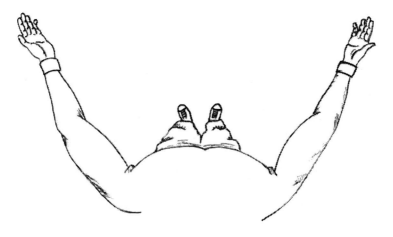

Fig.1

Clearly, with one look, it is the opposite. And to prove it, I have only to compare this First-Person-Singular body with those other second- and third-person bodies. Taking exactly what is presented—which is to see from the First-Person perspective—all other bodies are right-side-up and headed, while this body is undeniably upside-down and headless. This body, my resurrection body—with arms outstretched to infinity, the enormous torso, truncated legs and little feet, the grass, the buildings, the mountains and sky—this is my true body, all of it here in this vast emptiness, an emptiness that is aware capacity for all that passes through. You have a face over there, but here my face is the scene, vibrant and alive, changing moment by moment.

Can you not say the same? Are you really what others see from where they are, or are you what you see from where you are? How could they know, when only you can say? Only you can see what a truly sensational body you have. It's called *Everything*.

BRAINLESS VEGETABLES

Don't you ever worry about being brainwashed by the Dharma? *What if none of it is true?*

Well, you could say that none of it *is* true. And you don't have to worry about brainwashing if you don't have a brain.

Very funny.

I didn't mean it that way. I meant, being brainwashed is not a concern for Who You Really Are. Here, there is no brain—no head! Nothing to get in the way of exactly what is, as it is. It's immediate. It's brainless, if you will.

See, that's what I mean about brainwashed. Everyone's got a brain, and without one we'd be vegetables.

What I Am is prior to a brain, prior to a head, prior to any object whatsoever. All objects appear *within* What I Am.

Here's the problem, and it's the difference between First-Person and third-person perspectives: Science takes the view of the third-person, and a third-person is a separate thing in a particular location inside a much larger thing called a world. In order to explain the interaction of the two, there has to be communication between them, and so we have the story of incoming stimuli, waves and particles meeting sense receptors, electro-chemical messages to brains that process them, then the reverse process as a reaction, and so on. Cause and effect. It accounts perfectly for all that appears to happen between third-persons and other objects in the world, but it doesn't account for "knowing," how one actually *experiences* anything.

For the First-Person, there are no presumptions that what applies there, applies here. Here, it's Pure Experience. There are no eyes that see, no ears that hear, no nose that smells or tongue that tastes, no brain that runs the show. Here, there is no separation between one object (a "me") and other objects (the world). There is only this vast and fully awake Emptiness within which the world dances, so that I am all things, just as they are, moment by moment. It's very colorful.

Thoughts also?

Yes, thoughts and feelings, attached to whatever they are thoughts and feelings about. Not "my" thoughts and feel-ings—just thoughts and feelings appearing like everything else passing through, part of the scene, whatever it happens to be.

Okay, what about those carrot sticks on the desk I brought back from the chowhall?

What about them?

Well, according to you, there's no brain, and the scene is what you are.

So… So I'm the brainless vegetable you said I'd be?

You said it, not me.

Touché, my friend!

PAIN IN THE ASS

What I Am, also called Basic Space of Awareness, often seems to contract into what I am not, a separate individual, only human after all. But What I Am—Basic Space of Awareness—*never* contracts. Contraction happens *in* What I Am, is a manifestation of What I Am, and I am infinitely elastic, identifying with all levels of my hierarchy of appearances.

Much of the time I identify with my human level: I say I am a human being. But then I stub a toe, and for the moment I am so intently focused on the toe that I am the toe. At other times I may identify with my family or my country, and should they come under attack, even be willing to die in the name of either.

But of course, the truth regarding What I Am is much more far-reaching. The fact is, I Am, but I am nothing in particular. Or more precisely, I am everything: I am this Basic Space of Awareness entertaining whatever arises, which is, as it turns out, exactly what I am.

Lately, no one has called me a pain in the ass, but I have been that, too.

CHOICE WORDS

I heard you upset some people at the Buddhist meeting yesterday. What was that about?

I said that there is no such thing as choice.

Did the teacher say there was?

Yes. He was explaining the traditional teaching that, leading to this very moment, there are an infinite number of causes and conditions over which we have no control, but during the moment itself, or rather, at the last second, we can influence the course of future causes and conditions by our personal choice of action. He gave the example of cooking a poached egg. To produce the egg in this moment, there had to be a chicken, chicken feed, a farm, a biosphere, the formation of a continent, a planet, and so on. At each juncture there are an infinite number of conditions, and one concludes that it took the entire universe to come up with that egg. But it wouldn't become a poached egg unless in those final seconds you decided to boil it for three minutes.

And you disagree?

I don't disagree with the concept of causes and conditions extending to infinity, I disagree with the concept of individual choice.

Why? It sounds reasonable to me.

It sounds reasonable to you because you think you're separate from the whole. But is that true?

Well, I see what you're getting at, but there are two worlds here—an ultimate world and a relative world, and it's the relative world in which we live and have the ability to choose.

No, there are not two worlds. We don't even live in *one* world, never mind two. The world and the "we" you refer to live in THIS—What You Really Are.

Okay, but how can you teach this to members of the sangha, *especially new members, who have no idea what you're talking about?*

But why teach what isn't true? Why perpetuate the very ignorance that Buddhism hopes to dispel?

Because you have to lead people gently into this. You can't just lay it all out there at once and expect them to understand, not without years of Dharma *training and meditation. They'll run away.*

Tell the truth, and it will be heard. It may be rejected, but it will be heard by That Which Knows.

That won't work.

And how well do current methods work? Are there millions of Buddhists waking up?

But look what happened at the meeting. People got upset with you. That kind of resistance can't possibly help... By the way, what did happen at the meeting?

I made the statement that it *all* has to go. I saw it as a case of teaching causes and conditions beyond one's control—presumably to demonstrate that there are no self-existing things—but then at the last second saying, "Wait a minute—if I let that concept run to its logical conclusion, it'll rid me of *me* too, so I'd better introduce the idea of choice into it, right at the end, where I am. Then I'll be safe."

And what was the reaction from others when you said it all had to go?

Everyone started talking at once. Someone said that choice is what distinguishes us from animals. Another claimed we'd all be nihilists and depressed if what I said were true. Another accused me of pretending to be awake.

What did you say to that?

About pretending to be awake? I wasn't able to respond because the teacher interrupted with the same idea you brought up a few moments ago—that there are two worlds: an ultimate and a relative.

So are you pretending to be awake?

As what you see here, as this body-mind, it's all conditioning, and in that sense, all pretense. As What I Really Am, however, there is only Awakeness, and no such thing as pretending or not pretending.

So they jumped all over you.

Sure. People don't like to hear that they're naked, that they're not who they think they are. And when you take away their concept of choice, you take away their clothes, you leave them with no sense of separate self. "You mean, things are happening and I have nothing to do with it? You mean, I'm just another cog in the infinite wheel of causes and conditions?"

It is depressing, isn't it!

Well, it's not true. The so-called infinite wheel of causes and conditions is an appearance, and it appears *inside* of What You Are. The source of depression is the false sense of self. Without that, you are the miracle of whatever is, just as it is.

So you think it's better just to give a person what tradition- ally has been considered the highest teaching, what has been reserved for those who are well along the path to enlightenment?

That would be second best.

Oh? What's first?

Show them. Let them see for themselves. Tell them not to take anybody's word about anything, but to *see* what they are, where they are. Where they have always been. Where they have never left.

The pointing exercise? *

Yes. Or the tunnel. Or the card. Anything whereby aware- ness is aware of awareness: boundless, empty, filled with the world, wide awake, and right here.

Looking within, the question of choice or no choice seems trite, doesn't it?

---

* For the pointing exercise and additional awareness exercises developed by Douglas Harding and friends, see the Headless Way website at www.headless.org.

Is the question even there?

Well, no, it isn't. There's just empty Presence filled with the scene.

Stay with that.

PURE SUBJECTIVITY

In fact, there are no objects. All is Subject. This is why objects are said to be "empty." They are *not*, as objects. They are Subject. This is why objects are said to have no intrinsic existence. Everything (appearing as anything) is Pure Subjectivity.

"You"—the body-mind you identify with—are one such object. That is why you are said to be "empty." You are not, as an object. You are Subject. This is why you are said to have no intrinsic existence, for you are Pure Subjectivity.

There is no separate individual, no separate "thing" anywhere. This is why all is said to be "void." Everything is Pure Subjectivity, functioning as apparently separate things— you, me, and the universe. Everything is Who I Really Am, and anyone can say the same.

THIS IS THE PATH

What's the difference between the direct path and the long, drawn-out path that some gurus teach?

Let's see... One is direct, and the other is long and drawn-out?

Nice answer. What I mean is, is the direct path the true teaching, the highest wisdom, and if so, why doesn't everybody go straight for that?

I don't know why anybody does anything, and anyway, there is actually no difference between the direct path and the long, drawn-out path. They only appear different to someone who checks his calendar.

But the non-duality message is the path whereby enlightenment can happen in a flash, while all the other paths can take lifetimes.

Yes, but you see, you're coming from the point of view of a "someone" who has "lifetimes," when actually you are no one who has nothing of the sort. The direct path and the prolonged path are both expressions of that no one, both paths come from That and return to That and never were anything *but* That. What we're talking about here is unmitigated Oneness, and by "unmitigated" I mean that it's not even One. It's Blazing Awareness, appearing just for the hell of it as direct path or long, drawn-out path or whatever else it dreams up.

Just for the hell of it?

Well, maybe it would have been better to have said, "Just for the heaven of it." But yes, it's spontaneous manifestation. We add the time, we add the story. And that's part of it, too. Space/time and story and "we" are all Blazing Awareness, manifesting. Pretending to be "other" but actually manifesting as Itself.

But why?

I don't know, maybe It likes to play with Itself.

. . . .

Why are you shaking your head?

You didn't have to put it that way.

Too profane?

Yeah... I mean, this is a serious matter. It's...

Holy?

Well, maybe not holy, but to me and to lots of others it's a matter of great importance, and not something to talk trash about.

Okay, let's use the word *lila*, the word Hindus use for this great play of life, this miraculous net of jewels each reflecting all the others, what Meister Eckhart called "God boiling within Himself," Self and other as One, playing two. So, to answer your question, it's *lila*.

I'm not getting anywhere with this.

That's the point! You're not getting anywhere anyway! The path is from here to here. There's never been a path *in* because you've never been *out*. There's never been a path *home* because you've never been *away*. *This* is the path!

That's what you're trying to do, isn't it—frustrate me!

This can be frustrating when you think you're separate from Oneness. The good news is, you're not, and even the "thinking you're separate from Oneness" is Oneness, thinking it's separate. At this point, to talk "path" with you would be to deceive you. We're been through the "path" thing before, and my guess is that you have some ego-investment as to where you are on the wisdom ladder, either high on the non-dual "direct" rung or down on the "lower" rungs of prolonged teachings. They are not different. They were never different. Who you think you are isn't doing it anyway. It's just Basic Space of Awareness, Primordial No-thing, showing up moment by moment as whatever, including the sense of being a separate self and the stories that flourish around that. It's all Awareness knowing Itself, and that's all.

A QUESTION OF ACCEPTANCE

There is the question of acceptance. You accept this, you accept that, you allow "what is," you "go with the flow"—and then a car flattens your cat and you stand at the curb spitting obscenities at the driver.

Then comes the guilt. Not so much for leaving the door open so the cat could bolt into the street, but for the obscenities, the lost composure, your lack of acceptance. So you eventually calm down and start over, accepting this, accepting that, going with the flow.

But here's a question God might ask: "What's to accept?"

In other words, you, the cat, the car, the driver, all the "this's" and "that's"—the entire flow—not only appears *in* God, it *is* God. Even the accepting is Him, accepting.

"Abiding" might be a better word. Abiding in "what is" because, after all, you *is* "what is"!

Or how about, instead of passively accepting "what is," you *actively choose* it? Then you might not only accept the you you think you are, but *be* the You you really are: the One Chooser of All! Not to mention that which is chosen.

LIFE IS JUST A BOWL OF CHERRIES

The last time we met, you said that being What Is is easy, while believing in a separate self is hard work. I experience just the opposite. For me, being What Is is not only difficult, it's impossible.

And yet it's what you are. You've never been anything else. The struggle begins when you believe you're a tiny segment of it, over here, in a body and up against all the rest of it, and from which you must somehow purchase a living. It's the story of this object called a "you" versus that object called "the world," and it's a big fat lie!

No, no. The struggle for me began when I got hooked on this spiritual quest. I've been on one path after another for eight years, and I don't seem to have gotten anywhere. You think meditation isn't hard? Or understanding some of this esoteric material—You think that's easy? The hardest part is when I have a relapse—like when I lose my temper and give up on this from time to time. Then for days or weeks I have to deal with guilt for not being able to handle whatever came up, like I know I should be above those things, but I'm not. Let me tell you, being spiritual is not easy. It's probably the hardest thing I've ever experienced.

Okay. We can go with that, if you want. But I don't think that's what you want.

No, it isn't. The strange thing is, I can't even drop this spiritual quest, although half the time I want to.

So what do you want from me?

I don't know. The truth, I guess.

All right, let's start again. The reason that What Is is easy is because what you are is not different from What Is anyway! There's nothing you can be or do that isn't What Is. So, the easy way to be or do anything is this way, as it is, right now. As others have said, "There is no path from here to here!" As for the past, it's gone, it doesn't exist. What was apparently done is done, and the way it appeared is exactly the way it was supposed to appear because that's the way it appeared! It couldn't have been any different. You can't change the past; nor, in fact, can you change the present or future. So relax and enjoy the ride. Be what you are, which is What Is.

Well ... that sounds easy, but doing it or being it is another matter. I can't ever seem to get in that free space. I never experience bliss, or anything like it. I hear the terms "joy" and "gratitude," and they're like foreign words to me. Part of the reason is that I don't have a guru and can't surround myself with sacred things, you know? If I were in an ashram or a monastery, it would be totally different. Maybe that's what I should do.

So your spiritual quest doesn't work, you can't drop it, and you still want to pursue it—is that what I'm hearing?

Yes, more or less.

Well, about all I can say is that I feel for you, because I know how painful that can be.

Is that all?

What more can I add that you won't hear anyway?

Tell me what to do.

You're doing it right now. You're breathing, you're digesting today's lunch, you're complaining about your spiritual quest.

What does that have to do with anything?

That's just it—nothing! Nothing has to do with anything ever! It just *is*, *is-ing*, and that's what you are and that's the only thing you can be said to be doing. There are no problems. Nothing about life or the world is hard except your thoughts about life and the world, and the thoughts aren't even yours.

What do you mean, they're not mine?

They come and go through you, within you, like anything else. They're clouds passing through the sky of Awareness, and you are Awareness. Memories, visualizations, imaginings of every sort appear as part of the world. Call them products of the brain, if you will, but what you call "brain" is also a product of the brain—and it's all appearance, all "out there" in the "world." What You Are is prior to thoughts, prior to memories and visualizations and anything having to do with brains, all of which appears within you and cannot appear without you.

Let me demonstrate the power of belief. Say you just woke up on this planet, were just born, and have no opinions or judgements about anything. You're like a baby, completely innocent. The only thing you can rely on is what is presently available, what you see and hear in the moment.

Now hold your glasses out in front of you at arm's length and slowly—very slowly—bring them forward, watching carefully what happens. Bring them in... Slowly... And now put them on.

What did you see?

The two lenses became one, like a monocle.

Yes. Looking back now, on your side of that monocle, are you looking out of two eyes, or one?

Well, I have two eyes, so...

On present evidence, do you have two eyes? Or are you looking out of one enormous eye, into which everything in the scene fits? What is your actual experience, regardless of what you believe?

Oh, I see what you mean. I'm looking out of one eye, and yes, it's huge. The glasses are huge, too—or the glass is. But still, I know I have two eyes...

In this present moment, *seeing what you see,* you experience not two eyes, but one—you said so yourself. For others, from their point of view, you have two eyes, while from yours, you don't. But instead of relying on what you see for yourself, you believe others, because this is what you learned as a child and are now deeply conditioned to believe. There is no way I could talk you out of this belief, and even though you see for yourself, right where you are and where no one else is, that it isn't true, you'll go on believing you have two eyes. Right now in this present moment—and every moment is the present moment—you experience what First-Person seeing is: one enormous, edgeless, empty, aware Eye, into which everything fits. It was Meister Eckhart who said, "The eye with which I see God is the same eye with which God sees me." In this present moment, without thoughts to back you up, look outside and tell me, is that object a "fence?" Who called that a "sky," and is that thing over there a "tree?" In fact, is anything "outside" or "over there," or is it here, all within this Eye?

So you're saying that everything in the world reflects thoughts and beliefs?

As who you think you are, seeing yourself from the third-person point of view—in other words, seeing yourself as others see you, which is how you are conditioned to see, and all the second-tier thoughts based upon that core belief, such as opinions and judgements—yes, you experience an untrue and therefore illusory world of separation, of confrontation, of longing, of strife. Seeing as First-Person, however, you experience it directly without separation, without judgement.

Without problems.

Yes. A fire happens on the stove, you move quickly to put it out—it's no problem. You lose your job, you notice you are searching for another—it's no problem. It's not difficult, there are no "should haves" or "shouldn't haves." Whatever shows up, whatever thoughts and feelings are attached to it, you see the rightness of it, the perfection in the moment. Never is there a problem—or let me put it this way—even problems are no problem for First-Person-Singular, Present Tense.

What is there then, numbness?

Good heavens, no! Look for yourself. Look from the single Eye that you are, and tell me if there is numbness.

Actually, things are a little sharper.

Yes. Awareness is aware of Awareness and the immediacy of what appears within it. Everything happens *in* you and *as* you, not *to* you.

Well, I got a small taste of what you mean, but I'll have to think about this.

You'd do better to look. By all means, question your beliefs— you may find them all to be untrue. But *seeing* what you are dismantles them altogether in that instant of recognition. Keep relying on what you see, and then see what happens to your beliefs.

PRIMORDIAL AWARENESS

Being nothing, no-thing, being, as it were, the pointless point, I am utterly still, unmoving, for I am empty of anything *to* move. Thus, I never go anywhere. Rather, everything goes through me, *as* me, and in this way I am all that moves.

Being nothing, no-thing, being the pointless point, I never *do* anything, for there is no one here to do it. And yet all that is done is done within me, *as* me, and in this way I am the sole doer.

Being nothing, no-thing, being the pointless point, I know only nothing. Here, there is nothing to know, and no mind to know it. I am Alert Unknowing, *in* which and *through* which pass all thoughts and what they are thoughts about. I am no-mind, and yet all that is known is what I am, and in this way I am One Mind, knowing all.

I am Primordial Awareness manifesting as Everything possible.

INVISIBLE MAN

Suppose I tell you that I definitely exist, that I have a mind and I inhabit this body and I am absolutely real, would you believe it?

No.

But you've said it yourself, things like, "Don't rely on anyone else's estimation of what you are from where they are, rely on what you see from where you are," and "Look for yourself, don't believe what others say you are." So I'm telling you that what I am is this body and mind and you don't honor that.

I do honor the thoughts, but I don't believe them.

Why?

Because I see Who I Am. Because what you are is Who I Am, and Who I Am is what you are, and I am not. There's no one and nothing separate, and when you see this, everyone and everything becomes perfect, and perfectly obvious as the only reality there is. This is Who I Am, and how could I leave you out of the picture?

Talking to you is frustrating, because I never seem to get anywhere.

Where would you like to get?

I don't know, but sometimes it's like I'm talking to a mirror.

Of course. I'm your projection, nothing more, so you think I am what you think you are, which is absolutely real and inhabiting a body. Perhaps I don't meet your expectations?

Yeah, sometimes it's like there's nobody home.

Which can be frustrating, I understand. Who I Am is invisible. It's you who give me life and form as my projection; you are the only reality I have at the moment. This is how it is for you also, but you don't see it. You are invisible, and I am your reality. We can both say it: What I Am is invisible, for that which is invisible cannot be two. Only in appearance are we different, and ultimately, even this isn't so. This is why I say that what you are is Who I Am. It is also why I don't believe you when you say you're real and inhabiting a body. I know, first hand, who you are, because I am you.

NOBODY WITH TWO BODIES

I have two bodies, the body others tell me they see from where they are "over there," and the body I see from where I am here. The body others see from over there (and from where cameras record it) is one among seven billion, is separate from all the other bodies, is powerless in the face of colossal odds, and is right-side-up with a head on top. I need this body for one very important reason: It shows me what I am *not*. All praise to the bathroom mirror!

The body I see from here—my resurrection body—is completely different from the body others see from over there. For one thing, it is upside-down and headless. For another, it is all-inclusive. It is whole, in that it includes the whole world, with not a grain of anything left out. Only the All—quarks to galaxies—can be my true body, one and indivisible, exploding instant by instant from this empty awake Source where I once thought I had a head. Here is a drawing of my resurrection body: (fig.2. Overleaf)

Right now, looking at what I am looking out of, I die to the "old man" and am born again as the new. I am resurrected as the Whole of What I Am: all things in No-thing, forever and never.

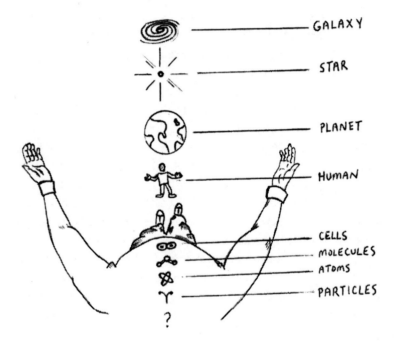

Fig.2

MORE IS LESS

Every day I learn a little more about enlightenment, so I guess I'm headed in the right direction. But then, the more I learn, the less I seem to know what it is personally, so it's like I end up right where I started. So before I know it, I'll probably know either everything about nothing or nothing about everything. Does that make sense?

Sounds to me like you figured out the unfigureoutable.

That's just it, I haven't figured out anything.

Instead of trying to learn *about* enlightenment, why not just look, and believe what you see? Do you have a face, or are you looking out of your Original Face, the one you had before you were born? All these words we toss around, when looking will say so much more. Believe what you see you are, right where you are, not what you've been told you are by others who are in no position to say, who are "over there."

But when I look, I see nothing, and there's nothing I can know about nothing.

Bravo! And everything comes and goes moment by moment in that nothing. That nothing is what you are, manifesting as everything. I could say, "manifesting as everything *sensed*," but that isn't the case. There's no something "here" sensing something else "there." It's just sights, sounds, smells, tastes, thoughts, feelings. Or better yet: seeing, hearing, smelling, tasting, thinking, feeling.

But where does all that come from?

It doesn't come from anywhere. There's nowhere it's not. And as for why, who knows? There's no need to figure out the unfigureoutable. Even the unfigureoutable can't figure itself out. It just is, and as I said, it's what you are. So why try to figure yourself out as if you were an object separate from yourself? You are Pure subjectivity, and everything that is, is That.

BLAMING AND SERVING

Blaming others and blaming oneself are the same. They are both "self" blaming "other," and "self" and "other" are not different.

Serving others and serving oneself are the same. They are both Self serving "other," and Self and "other" are not different.

However, the former is the result of the belief in a separate self, while the latter is the natural expression of the One Self, whether or not one knows it. Both are manifestations of the Absolute, but the former hurts, while the latter brings joy. Feelings rarely lie.

A QUESTION OF PURPOSE

You said that the purpose of life is to wake up.

I said that? I must have been having a bad day.

So that's not the purpose of life? What is, then?

That's a difficult question to answer because, as I've also said, it's all internal. There's no outside. In Oneness, everything is self-begotten, self-perpetuating, self-supported, self-motivated. There's nothing to get that's separate from Self.

Then there's no purpose whatsoever.

That's not true either. Purpose is everywhere. Those who say there is no purpose often say so quite purposefully. Life is full of purpose—of every sort. You could even say that life *is* purpose. It's magical, awe inspiring, don't you think?

I guess so, but it also seems a little depressing, the way you're describing it.

Depressing?

Yes, because you're saying that there's purpose within life, which is different than saying there's a purpose to life.

It's depressing, I take it, because you believe you're a separate self on a mission to reach or solve or somehow incorporate this so-called "purpose-to-life" and thereby "fulfill your destiny," as they say. It's depressing because you think you're *out* of Oneness and need a purpose-to-life to get back *in*. But this is what I'm saying: You were never, are not now, and never will be *out*. You, Who You Really Are, are the purpose to Yourself. God has, is, and fulfills His own destiny.

Or let's take a step back and put it this way: You've looked at what is looking and seen Emptiness at your core, Unborn Awareness. It's what you are, it's awake, it's boundless, and it's absolutely no-thing. It's intuited as Presence, or Being, but it has no objective qualities whatsoever. Here, as no-thing, there is no purpose, no choice, no anything. It's called Basic Space of Awareness, and that about describes it.

For the sake of understanding, we say that this Basic Space of Awareness, this no-thing, is "here," and everything else, the entire universe of *things*, including the body and thoughts and feelings and all that comes and goes, is out "there." We do this in order that we might see that our true identity is formless Awareness and not a body-mind, which, as I said, is one of the *things* out "there." So we point at where we assumed we had a face and *see* What We Really Are: empty awake Basic Space of Awareness, right here, right where we are, while everything we are aware *of* is out "there."

This duality of "here-there" is a step in the right direction, but it isn't the whole truth and is discarded when the identity shift has taken place from personal self to impersonal Self (or no-self). Seeing you are empty of anything, you also see you are filled with everything. The nature of Empty Awareness can be described as *Capacity*, awake Capacity for whatever appears and disappears. But as Capacity, it holds nothing, does nothing, thinks nothing, is nothing. It is Pure Consciousness, and not a glimmer of purpose resides there. Purpose, like everything else that comes and goes, is of the world. Here, as no-thing, I have no life—all of my life is over there in you, in everything that appears, moment by moment.

So nothing is left out. I am all of it, nothing and everything, No-thing/Everything as One, and thus to say, "There is no purpose" is correct, and to say, "There is purpose everywhere" is also correct, and this realization is said to be the purpose of life.

Somehow I think we're back where we started.

Yes, that happens, and not always on purpose!

WHAT'S THE MATTER WITH MATTER?

The crux of the problem seems to be our devotion to matter. We live in a material world where matter matters most. For example, the idea that matter produces consciousness is so commonplace as to be rarely challenged. You and I are said to be conscious because of a special degree of organization of nervous matter; in other words, consciousness is an "epiphenomenon," a by-product of brain processes.

This means, of course, that when the body dies, so do we. And it means that sentient beings, however many billion are deemed sentient, each have their own separate and special consciousness, tucked away in a head or some other body part where a brain resides. It means that you and I are not only solitary, we are less than inconsequential, the tiniest of specks ever-so-briefly flickering on and off in an unimaginably vast and impersonal universe. We are, like all of life, an impossible accident, at best.

The irony is that the current scientific consensus regarding matter is that it is anything but material! In fact, what is it, really? Condensed energy? But what is that? At the level of the very small, not only can I not say what matter is, I can't say it even exists. It is both particles and waves at the same time, is both here and everywhere at once, is a "probability function" dependent on the presence of an observer. And if I can't say what matter is, I can't say what I am. If consciousness comes from matter, it comes from nothing, organized or not.

But, you say, brain processes correlate perfectly with perceptions, thoughts, and feelings. Brains can be electrically stimulated to produce predictable mental images or physical reactions. An MRI can demonstrate without question that conscious activity is brain-based, and area-specific, at that.

The problem, I answer, lies in confusing the contents of consciousness with consciousness as the container. It may be a fact that brain processes correlate predictably with perceptions, thoughts, and feelings, but brains, like perceptions, thoughts, and feelings, are part of the world, and all of it is content, all comes and goes in consciousness. Consciousnesss —the container—is the nothing of which matter is made, the nothing at the heart of every material thing, quarks to galaxies, including the quarks, particles, atoms, molecules and cells of all brains. Consciousness is pure aware capacity for everything that fills it, moment by moment.

This means, by comparison, that what we really are— consciousness—is immortal, was never born and therefore never dies. It means that consciousness is one, that it is nothing and therefore that there is no such thing as multiple consciousnesses. It means that what we are is not only the center of the universe, it is the universe itself, consciousness appearing as a universe, anything and everything. It means that there are no accidents, no mistakes, and never have been. It also means that there is no "we," that there is only this solitary Presence, awake Capacity here and now for all that appears there and then.

Matter is simply consciousness, appearing as matter. What's the matter with that? Why, No-thing at all!

LOUSY DINNER PARTIES

What do you want?

Nothing.

But everybody wants something.

That's the joke. First, everybody already has what they want, and second, what they have is what they are. Besides, there is no "everybody."

Would you explain that?

How can you want something outside of yourself when there is no outside of yourself? You think you want something, but you *are* it. Everything you see, hear, taste, touch, or think of, you are. So what is there to *get*, and how could that improve you? All you are is the wanting, and not even that.

Then why do you buy food or clothing or take a shower or visit a friend—or do anything, for that matter?

It happens of its own accord. There's no need involved. I *am* all those things as they appear.

Let's talk in terms of everyone—or at least of me and everyone I know. We all need or want something, nearly all the time. To say otherwise would be a lie.

You *think* you need something because you think you're a separate someone up against other someones and living in a separate and predominantly hostile world. It's the same old story, and while it appears to be true, if you go within, if you investigate, you may discover it's not. All the things you think you want—power, fame, and fortune—are all substitutes for what you really want, which is simply to be what you are, and none of the things you think you want will give you more than a moment's worth of what you really want. The joke is, you already *are* what you want, right now, right where you are.

What do you mean, "investigate"?

Take a look at thoughts, for starters. You've learned that they belong to you, that they're personal, but they're not. Thoughts make up the world projected as "other," and as such are inseparable from the things they are thoughts about, and are therefore no more than appearances. All my life I believed that the thoughts I experienced were *my* thoughts, were who I was, and I couldn't see them for what they were. Question each thought. Find out if it is true, and see how it colors your experience. Do this as if you were an infant who hasn't yet been told who or what it is, or what anything is. Get to the root of thought, the root of language, where innocence lies, and discover what you *really* are, which is prior to thought.

It's impossible for me not to see the world as separate. I can't go back to being an infant!

You can't be an infant, but you can consciously see from the point of "don't know." Putting aside your beliefs, going only on present evidence, you can see that what you are *includes* the world, that even the things you *think* you want you already have, and moreover, already are.

For instance, relax and allow awareness to take in awareness—look back at the transparent no-thing that you're looking out of, and notice how wide it is, how everything easily fits within it: You literally hold the sky and mountains and town below, the fence and yard, the buildings nearby and everything close at hand—all of it *within* this empty awareness that you are. To say that you *own* these things is a gross understatement: They are *inside* of you, are part of you; are, in fact, what you are. How much more convincingly could you possess them?

If, for instance, I drop this pencil in your hand and say it's yours, how is it that you own it? Look at your hand, look at the pencil. They are both "things," both solidly up against one another. You could just as easily say that the pencil owns the hand, as the hand owns the pencil. But notice that they are both within this clear awareness, this awake capacity and what it is capacity for, void and form alike. When this is seen, in that moment the game is over, the question of ownership and what it can do for you is no longer a question, and there remains only What You Are.

I do see what you mean—how awareness and everything that fills it are inseparable—but it makes no sense that this is what I am. Everything that fills it is continually changing. How can I be that?

Pure awareness never changes, never moves, is stillness itself. That which appears within it is everything that could ever appear, in continuous movement and variety. This inseparable pair is about as close as one can get to an explanation of what one is. And incidentally, the two would not be the same if they didn't appear as opposite, and neither are anything at all! You can't be nothing and you can't be something, so give up the idea of being this or that or anything. But of course, you can't do that either.

Because there's no separate "me" to do it?

Exactly.

Then I'm really in a quandary... Or is it that a quandary is in me?

The latter sounds closer to the truth.

Well... What were we talking about? Oh yes—about wanting. Hmm, right now there doesn't seem to be much to say about that, does there? Or anything else, for that matter.

I think it was Wayne Liquorman, AKA Ram Tzu, who said that awakening makes for lousy dinner parties.

Yes, I can see why.

FIRST-PERSON-SINGULAR BODY

How do I know that my true body is this "single-eyed, wide-armed and all-inclusive Resurrection body"?[1] How do I know that I wear the world-body of First-Person-Singular?

Because I need all of my levels to be What I Am. Certainly I need my "interior" levels, the particles, atoms, molecules, and cells that make up this upside-down flesh body. And certainly to be human I need other humans. And certainly I need the biosphere and my planetary and solar and galactic levels, for what body could do for a second without air and water and life, or the earth or sun or Milky Way?

The fact is, as First-Person-Singular, I can't get along without every last bit of the All of it, each part as precious as the next, no matter how ugly or mean it appears. This is my body—Everything—all right here, and as First-Person-Singular, all levels are my interior levels because I am not in the world, the world is in me. Because the One needs the whole to be whole.

[1.] D.E. Harding, in *To Be And Not To Be*, London, Watkins, 2002.

SHEER GENIUS

Why isn't this direct teaching more available?

Available to whom?

To everyone.

That's just it—as First-Person Singular, there is no "every-one." It's like the Bodhisattva Vow. The bodhisattva vows not to take enlightenment until all others are enlightened. But to a bodhisattva, there *are* no others! It is said that upon the Buddha's enlightenment, all beings were enlightened. It's an odd thing, this teaching others, when there are no others to teach. So the term "more available" doesn't make sense.

Yes, but to some, what you just said is frustrating. It's like, there's no way to learn this without a teacher or a teaching, and yet you're saying there's nothing to teach. So what does a person do, just give up?

That would be a beginning. But give up what?

Give up trying to understand. Give up listening to the teaching.

Better to give up being a person. Then there's no need to listen to the teaching.

You're like a walking koan, you know it?

You can say that again! I never could figure myself out.

But really, it seems that if more people heard the direct message instead of what they hear in the typical religious message, there might be a lot more enlightened beings on this planet. And that could result in a more peaceful world, not to mention a greener planet.

Amen.

You agree?

You seem surprised.

Well, yes, I guess I am. I didn't expect you to so readily agree.

Because?

Because you usually like to point out... Because I probably said some things that were...

Nonsense?

Yeah.

Like what? Tell me again the "But really" part.

Ha ha! I can't. It's pretty funny, isn't it! As if there could be something wrong with the planet. As if there could be enlightened beings, for that matter.

That *is* hilarious!

So the whole teacher and teaching thing is a farce? And yet it seems to have worked for some, or so I've heard.

Yes, you said it all in the word "seems." Teacher and teaching, paths to enlightenment, people waking up—all of this is a product of the Absolute, doing "life." It's all appearance. In fact, no one has ever been asleep. Nor has anyone been enlightened. There's no separate, self-existing being to do or be either.

And yet, some will hear this, see what they really are, and wake up.

Yes. Isn't that amazing!

I'll tell you what worked the best for me, and that was when you led me through Harding's pointing exercise. After that, I knew what all the teachings were alluding to. It is, as you said, the shift from The Word to The Vision. If there's a direct path, pointing and looking has to be it. And it's not really a path, is it? It's more like an arrival. It's... I don't know, what would you say it is?

Sheer genius.

Yes. That sounds good. Sheer genius.

BIG WHEEL

I am both the hub and the rim of the universe. I am the still
Center and all that turns about me.

Sometimes I am asleep at the wheel, pretending to be a
tiny part and nothing else, and then I awaken to see that I
am the wheel itself, wheeling within myself, as myself.

Truly I am a Big Wheel, and THIS is how I roll.

LURKING

Can you ever go back to being a separate self?

And believe it? No.

So you're sort of "out there" forever?

Out where? I've always been right here. I couldn't be anywhere else because there's nowhere I'm not!

*Doesn't that frighten you a little? You know, not being able to
get outside of yourself, knowing that everyone and everything is
only you?*

From the point of view of a separate self, it can be frighten-
ing. But there is only What Is, and What Is is What I Am.
How could I frighten or be frightened of myself?

So it's like that forever?

There's no forever. Forever is a dream-concept. Space-time
is a construct, and What You Are is spaceless, timeless,
aware Emptiness, dreaming a space-time universe that goes
on "forever."

Okay, so let me ask you this: Can you pretend *to be a separate
self?*

Pretend to be a thing separate from all the other things, like
a tree, say, or a cardboard box, or maybe a human being?
No. I can, however, lurk.

Lurk?

Hide. Wait. And at the right moment, such as during this conversation, I may meet Myself in you.

But how?

Because What I Am is not two. What I Am is absolutely nothing, appearing as everything. As absolutely nothing, we cannot be different. We are I, Aware No-thing. What I Am is appearing now as you, playing the role of a separate self, but I know it's only a role. So it's in you that I pretend. You are all the pretence I can muster, while What I Am lurks, waiting.

Waiting for what?

For Myself, of course. For you to knock on the door and discover you are already inside. For you to be what you already are, which is I, What I Am.

Frankly, I'm not sure I'm ready for that.

And so I lurk.

WHAT THE...?

What am I?

Obviously I am not my name, my job, my reputation, my address, my connection to family, race, nationality or planet. So what am I?

I could be this body, but on which level? Comprised of over ten billion cells, the cells comprised of molecules, the molecules of atoms, the atoms of particles, I seem to be a walking probability function, not really here in the material sense.

Am I my thoughts? God help me if I am! All these fleeting memories, concerns, conjectures, scenes, dreams, observations, conclusions, expectations, contemplations, ruminations—it's enough to drive me batty, if I believe them. And who is this "me" to go batty, this "I" to believe or not believe them? What about that thought? Is it any different than the others? Even though this "me" thought seems more stable, more available, doesn't it come and go like the rest, slipping in and out of nowhere?

Perhaps the "me" idea comes from you over there, what you or a camera or a mirror "sees." At a distance of ten feet, you and the camera and the mirror say I am a human being. But what if you are a mile away? Am I then a speck? What if I hang a giant mirror in the sky? Am I a town, a continent, a planet? What I appear to be to you—is that what I am?

Well then, maybe if I'm anything at all, I'm all of it. I am, in other words, the whole package, all my apparent levels, particles to galaxies. Maybe I have to be everything to be anything.

But what just came up with that sentence? For instance, have I decided to write about my parts, or have my parts decided to write about themselves? Have these ten billion cells, each one a living being in its own right, conspired to write this autobiography, or was it the world of the even smaller that came up with these words? Where the heck am "I" in this picture?

There is, it would seem, no footing. I can't say I'm anything, and therefore I might say I'm nothing. Or perhaps I should say I'm everything. But being nothing and being everything is not the same as not-being-anything. Or maybe it is.

TWO TO TANGO

All the spiritual traditions describe some form of surrender to a higher power, but you've said there's no such thing as surrender. How do you figure?

In the first place, there's no separate, self-existing one to surrender or not surrender. And surrender to whom or to what? Wholeness is wholeness.

What about surrendering the false self?

Again, wholeness is wholeness. The irony is, the so-called "false self" sets itself up as the one who will surrender. That way it gets to continue being a "false self," and of course, surrender never happens. But this is only wholeness, playing the game of parts.

But why can't the false self surrender?

I told you already.

All right, there's no separate one who can surrender, and the false self is just an idea, a mistaken identity—I understand that. But it seems to me that this false self might surrender itself to this understanding, to seeing it isn't the real Self.

Well, let's follow that. As you said, there's certainly plenty of history behind that notion. My guess is that spiritual leaders, when asked about awakening, offered descriptions that followers quickly turned into methods. Out of a sentence or two, thousands of years of devotion and sacrifice followed, including the idea of surrendering the false self to a higher power. This is the way of the world, of appearance, which, as I said, is wholeness expressing itself as parts. But there is only wholeness, so in reality there is no surrender because, as they say, it takes two to tango.

Wholeness or not, I don't see how you can deny the idea of surrender. In my experience, especially in A.A., surrender happens.

I'm not denying the *idea*, the appearance of it. I'm saying that it doesn't really happen, isn't needed, isn't "real." Every idea, every thing, is an expression of wholeness, and therefore *is* wholeness. Wholeness thinks all the thoughts and plays all the parts. All happenings are wholeness, appearing to happen. And incidentally, I've no doubt that surrender works for you.

Now you've reversed yourself!

No, I haven't.

You just said that surrender works! Am I going crazy or are you? Why do you say this stuff, then change up?

To piss you off?

No, I don't think so. You do this for a reason, and eventually I'll figure it out.

No, there's no reason. And I didn't change up. And when you figure out the unfigureoutable, let me know and we'll both celebrate.

EGO

The ego, the story of a separate self as a body and mind, is not to be discarded, not to be subdued, not thought of as a mistake. Personal uniqueness need not be dropped. After all, is not the sense of "I am" the thrust, the life force, the liveliness of the universe?

The problem with the ego is not that it's self-centered, it's that it's not self-centered enough. It's *off* center, identified with a particular thing in a world of everything. Here, at the center of the universe, a center into which the entire universe fits with ease, the ego, "I Am," this unmistakable sense of Being, is no-thing-at-all, an emptiness so absolutely empty it makes room for everything. This is the true ego, the truly self-centered ego, and all that appears, quarks to galaxies, is what it is, loving itself.

Released from the confines of the body and mind and allowed to fly to the limit where it belongs, the ego is alive and well and intensely personal. It is What You Are: empty, boundless, aware, and filled with your true body—the universe. It is the One Being of All.

Be that. You are anyway.

TWO SCHOOLS, NO PATH

One of the topics of the meeting last week was the two schools of enlightenment in Ch'an Buddhism, the sudden school and the gradual school. I seem to be a member of the gradual school, but I've heard you say that enlightenment is instantaneous, or sudden.

The two schools date back to the T'ang Dynasty in China, and I believe the gradual school was referred to as the school of "deliverance," which could be thought of as a long process of slowly eliminating conditioned beliefs and finally arriving at a point of understanding, or readiness, beyond which one cannot conceptually go. Thus, one is "delivered" to the gate. But because there is no solution of continuity, no way to pass through to the other side conceptually, you end up no closer to enlightenment than you were at the start. In other words, the school of deliverance in no way guarantees delivery.

However, I've read that the true meaning of deliverance intended by the T'ang Dynasty masters had to do not with understanding *prior* to enlightenment, but with understanding *after* enlightenment. Deliverance was the filling in, the picking up of the pieces, learning to function in the world of appearance while fully aware that nothing is what it seems, that all is only Awareness manifesting as the "ten thousand things."

So enlightenment is always sudden.

In a manner of speaking, yes. Enlightenment isn't a process. Nirvana and samsara, although seen to be identical, are entirely different and do not relate causally. Samsara is conceptual, and no amount of addition or deduction, no manner of thinking or doing will result in nirvana, defined as that which is beyond thinking and doing.

Picture samsara as our three-dimensional world of appearance, and nirvana as a further dimension perpendicular to the three, so that nirvana is at right angles to and unavailable to our perceptual/conceptual apparatus, and yet, just as the higher third dimension includes within it the lower two dimensions, the higher dimension of nirvana includes within it the three dimensions of samsara. From the perspective of a one-dimensional point, a two-dimensional plane can never be known. Likewise, from a two-dimensional plane, a tri-dimensional world of volume can never be known. Nor can the further and non-conceptual dimension of our example—nirvana—be known from the perspective of our three-dimensional world of objective appearance. Subject cannot know itself objectively, because it is what is objectivizing. Nirvana appears *as* samsara, and for that reason cannot know itself *from* samsara.

What I'm left with, then, is not exactly good news. I've been following this path for years, and I find out from you that it no more leads to enlightenment than if I'd been digging ditches.

But the good news is that there's never been a "you" to be enlightened or not enlightened. It's all been a simple misunderstanding: Thinking you're a separate "someone" is a fabrication of mind, and therefore unreal. You are no-thing, and deliverance cannot deliver no-thing anywhere. What you are as no-thing is everywhere at once, and because there is nowhere you're not, you're already there!

That said, it can also be said that the gradual school has its merits. Enlightenment happens when it happens. It may come at the end of a long period of spiritual preparation—meditating and studying for apparent lifetimes—or it may come totally unannounced. In the latter case, without a cultural or spiritual context to support it, it might be dismissed as a physical or mental anomaly, or interpreted as pathological, a dissociative disorder. No-self in a Buddhist monastery is not the same as no-self on a psychiatrist's couch.

Then it's better to live in a culture that supports it, like India with its tradition of wandering holy men. Or to at least be a member of a spiritual community here that will recognize it for what it is.

Yes, that may be true, but even in India and elsewhere there seems to be an extended period of adjustment, or deliverance, after enlightenment. It's a matter of re-entry, or re-connection, of returning to apparent normalcy and relating to others, knowing all the while that there are no "others," acting "as if."

But not intentionally deceiving others.

No, no. It happens without intent. It's simply a function of THIS, relating to Itself, meeting confusion and misunderstanding at its own level. It's the bodhisattava's return. It's been termed compassion, but sometimes it's just plain surprise.

Surprise at what?

That it appears as "other." That "other," which is Itself, appears to misunderstand, appears to think it's separate. Sometimes it's so comical it's hard not to laugh.

But sometimes there's fear. Do you think the gradual path helps to prevent or at least minimize fear?

Maybe, maybe not. I've heard of people who were steeped in spiritual practice, who had been meditating for decades, but when it came to loss of self, were abruptly thrown into panic. And I know of others who had had no spiritual training whatsoever, and after spontaneously waking to no-self, knew only peace. There seems to be no formula for this, and I think the message is clear: What the illusory self appears to do or not do has no bearing on What Is.

Well, the message I'm getting is mixed. On the one hand I hear you say that deliverance has a part to play, even if only indirect. And on the other hand you say that deliverance has no bearing at all, that it doesn't relate to enlightenment.

Deliverance can't wake you up. What you are is Timeless Aware Emptiness, dreaming a "me" that appears to "last" over a period of "time" constituting a "life." And in this dream the "me" character has the notion that if it participates in a process of spiritual development it will be delivered to the mysterious land of enlightenment, where all is rosy and neat. But this is a dream. And there is nothing in the dream (which is conceptual, objective, horizontal) that can influence Timeless Aware Emptiness (which is non-conceptual, non-objective, vertical) any more than a shadow can influence its host. Timeless Aware Emptiness is perfect. It needs nothing, and is not the result of anything. Nothing comes before it and nothing comes after, and no dream character or dream process can affect it because it's simultaneously the Dreamer, the Dreaming, and the Dreamed.

And yet the dream goes on.

Yes.

Okay, I think I've got it. Deliverance can't wake me up, but it may help the illusory dream character after awakening, because the dream goes on. Is that it?

No, but it sounds good.

Then what... ?

It can't be neatly explained. It can be *seen,* but never explained. And when it is seen, it is seen by no-one, which is Itself. That's about as close as we can come by way of explanation, and already we've said way too much.

MAGNUM OPUS

Are you creative? Are you an artist or a composer? Suppose it were revealed to you that you were the Center and the Origin of the universe, that the aware Capacity you're providing the scene *is* the scene, and therefore that the universe could not exist without you? Could anyone be more creative? Is there an artist or a composer who could match your creativity, considering that you created *them*?

Seeing and being Who You Really Are is not a passive affair. It is not a case of being the "witness," the observer of "what is." It is a matter of being both the observer and the observed, as *one*. The creation, all of creation, is you—and here's the stunner: You are no one! If anyone, you are everyone. If anything, you are everything. For everyone and everything are all you can be said to be, and since that leaves out anyone and anything else, well, you've created it all!

And such a masterpiece! How do you do it? What's more, how do you create *Yourself*? That you create the universe is one thing, but that you create Yourself is another. There could be simply nothing, a blank, but here you are: awake, conscious, moment by moment lifting Yourself out of the abyss of nowhere by your own bootstraps, completely unaided and for no apparent reason but to *be*. Compared to that, all else is effortless, indeed!

Who are you? Have you noticed that you're the One Creator Itself?

ALL AND NOTHING

We were talking about deliverance last time, and you said that deliverance can happen before or after enlightenment. Assuming that deliverance means the same as path, I can't see how there can be a path after enlightenment. Call it "re-entry" or whatever, it makes no sense from the point of view of "now."

You're perfectly right. A path only manifests in hindsight, and it stretches back to infinity. We were conversing from the "guest" position, whereas if we had been in the "host" position, there would have been no talk of a path.

What is this "guest" versus "host" position?

Simply another way to distinguish samsara from nirvana, and of course, from the perspective of nirvana, the two are not different.

All these terms can be confusing.

Yes, you're right about that, too. We try to use words that best convey the meaning of what ultimately can't be conveyed, and sometimes they cause only more confusion. But please continue, because I see that you're on to something here.

Well, it occurred to me that because enlightenment happens to no one and is outside the concept of time, from that vantage point a path must necessarily be prior to enlightenment.

A path is, of course, part of what comes and goes. It's an appearance in Awareness. And with that in mind, it may be viewed as illusory. But it is also seen as This-Which-I-Am, appearing, and seen in this way from the "host" position, it really is quite extraordinary, considering that I, as What I Am, orchestrate it all.

I read Harding's example of traveling on a country road and stopping at an inn for a cup of coffee. His point was that the entire universe, every last molecule of it, had participated in bringing that cup of coffee to him at exactly that moment, and he traces the connections backwards in time from the waitress to the inn and innkeeper, to the delivery truck, to the distributor, to the ship, to the plantation in South America, to the coffee plant, the soil, the rainfall, sun, galaxy, etcetera—as well as the infinite number of causes and conditions branching out horizontally from each of those points along the way.

Yes, the whole thing, as a whole, is the path. From the host position it is seen that everything—not just the spiritual practice, but all of appearance, the entire history of all there is—is the path, and it leads to right here, right now.

Including the "re-entry" after, the "picking up of the pieces," as you said?

Yes, it's all in hindsight. How could it be otherwise?

There's gratitude in seeing this.

Most definitely! Gratitude for this gift of a universe, from no one, to no one, from Itself to Itself, free and clear.

There's also humility, in the sense that I had nothing to do with it.

Yes, no option. A separate "you" has no option, and humility is synonymous with "no separate you." Not my will but

Thine, O Lord. Path, seen in this manner, is the divine path, love in action, the manifestation of benevolence, and it includes everything that ever happened, intricately and intimately connected in oneness.

And yet there is no path?

No. It's truly amazing, isn't it? There's this incredible path leading to right here and right now, and it's all appearance, which is to say that in reality there is no path, never has been, and never will be. Absolutely everything happens, and absolutely nothing happens, and they are the same!

Whew! That's hard to digest.

Impossible to digest. It's either seen or not seen.

I've been thinking about something else you said—that my real body is the universe. This more or less brings me to the same conclusion as having a path does.

That, for instance, you have no body? That the universe is actually Awareness, manifesting as a universe?

Yes. It "delivers" me to the gate; it takes me to that point where logic breaks down.

How does it go?

You should know. It was you who first brought it up.

Remind me, then.

Well, because of Einstein's mass-energy equation, I know that all material objects are merely forms of condensed energy. Also, learning from science that matter is made up of smaller and smaller parts such that, the smaller they are, the more indistinguishable they are, I conclude therefore that there is no difference between what I call "my" body—this body of flesh—and all the matter around it, so that, ultimately, there is no matter "around" it because it is all my body. Where does my body end and the chair begin? The air in the room, the desk, the walls, the window—all of it, every object in the room, and the room itself, are composed of the same essence, and there is no break in the continuity of it—it goes out from here to infinity, and I call it the "universe." It's all me. So it's like, everywhere I look, I'm moving through myself. Or rather, myself is moving through me!

Yes, and you said it better than I did. It brings you to the gate, where there's nowhere to go, no way out.

And no room for anyone else.

Exactly. It's all You. You are the Alone.

Einstein and others must have seen this for themselves, no?

No doubt they did. Some said as much, in their own way. Not exactly a popular topic in the scientific community, however, and not a message that furthered anyone's career at the research lab.

So that many may have simply kept quiet about it?

Who would believe them anyway? And what would it matter to THIS, to What Is, The All?

Not a thing. And I say that as The All.

Wonderful! Thank you for that, and thank you for the reminder of Who I Am!

THE FOUR O's

1. OMNISCIENT: How, as Pure Subjectivity, am I omni-scient? I used to be a know-it-all. I thought I knew everything. Now, however, I have to say I know Nothing (No-thing), which turns out to be all there is to know about anything.

2. OMNIPRESENT: How, as Pure Subjectivity, am I omnipresent? I used to think I was something here, and everything else was over there. Now, however, I see I am both Nothing and Everything, all right Here, that there is no anywhere or anywhen I am not.

3. OMNIPOTENT: How, as Pure Subjectivity, am I omnipotent? I used to think I was a powerless speck in a vast and impersonal cosmos. Now, however, I see I am the Still Hub around which, in which, and as which this vast and intensely personal cosmos revolves. As Pure Subjectivity, everything that is created is created by Who I Am.

4. OMNIVOROUS: I'll eat anything.

SAY NO MORE

I've been in 12-Step programs for years, and what I've always liked about the 12-Step message is the emphasis on acceptance. It's one of the reasons I was attracted to Buddhism also—the idea of accepting whatever feelings or sensations that arise during meditation, not trying to change them or avoid them. It's a matter of surrender, when you come down to it, but I've heard you say that there's no such thing as surrender, so I'm wondering what your thoughts are on acceptance.

Well, the point is, as First-Person-Singular, Present Tense, as Oneness, as the Totality, who or what could surrender to whom? The same with acceptance. Your question assumes that there is someone or something apart from the Totality, and there isn't.

[Long pause]

And that's all you're going to say about it?

Already I've said too much. The Absolute is *absolute*. It's not partly absolute, needing acceptance from some other part. Wholeness is wholeness. Wholeness isn't halfness or quarterness or three-fifths of a gazillion. It's whole.

So why does just about every teacher from every spiritual tradition mention surrender and acceptance? Are they just making it up?

Not at all. Teachers are there to teach that something is missing, that something unknown needs to be known or something lost needs to be found. They are characters operating in the great drama of *lila*. Truly, there is nothing to teach. And the drama goes on.

But you're right. Every spiritual tradition has something to say about surrender, and most hold it in high regard. Surrendering to God, for instance, or surrendering one's will to that of God's. The direct route, or what surrender is really about, however, is a matter of total acceptance of "what is," every moment. By that I mean, *seeing what you are*, moment by moment. So that there is no separate "you" here accepting "what is" there; rather, "what is" is what you are! No separation. Total acceptance.

Frankly, I don't understand this direct route. The sort of acceptance I had hoped to hear about is more in line with what you said about surrendering to God.

Which is a good reason for it never to have been said.

So that's all?

That's all.

You aren't going to say any more?

No.

D.E. HARDING'S SCIENTIST ON A MISSION

I am a Harding scientist, which means that I take the evidence exactly as it is presented, and my mission is to find out what you are (whatever a "you" could be).

I am camped at the edge of the universe where I see nothing at all, only a vast emptiness, but I am equipped with a homing device that will lead me directly to you, although I have no idea what you will look like when I get there.

So I hop in my spaceship and, following the homing device, set out at warp speed toward you, wondering what I will encounter, if anything. Eventually I see a light in the distance, and, traveling closer, I see that the light is actually a spiral galaxy, so I think, "Ah, that's what you are—a galaxy!" But when I come up to you I lose your appearance as a galaxy and notice that the homing device is pointing at a particular star in the galaxy. "Oh, so you're a star," I conclude. But not so fast!—because when I approach, I see that the star is a solar system and that the homing device is pointing to one of the planets. "Well, you're not a star, after all, but a planet." Three times now I have been presented with different appearances of you, but when I went up to you, you turned out to be something else!

So you appear to be a planet, but sure enough, when I reach you, I lose your appearance as a planet and find that you are a continent, then a country, then a city, a house, and—"What in the world is that four-limbed creature standing on the porch that my homing device is pointing to?"

I decide, albeit with much hesitation, that maybe this is what you are—a human being. But then, why should I assume you are a human being when all of your other appearances were just that—appearances? So I approach, this time with magnifying instruments, and, just as before, you turn out to be something else entirely, an assemblage of sorts, an enormous city of living cells, billions strong. Closer still, you become one cell, then molecules, then one molecule, then atoms, then one atom, then particles—and now, having almost arrived according to the homing device, I am at a place where once again I see nothing at all, only a vast emptiness.

From this experiment I conclude that you are either all of the above or none of the above, that what you appear as depends solely on my (the observer's) distance from you, and furthermore, that whatever I go all the way up to, I lose altogether!

Fig.3

There is one problem, however. The homing device indicates that I have not quite reached you, and yet, taking one more step, it reads that I am receding from you. At this point it occurs to me to turn around and look out *with* you, and when I do, I see what you see, with all of your appearances, particles to galaxies, arrayed before you. The homing device shuts off, and I realize that I have not only found you, I *am* you.

I conclude that, whatever I go all the way up to, there I am—Pure Aware Emptiness, appearing as anything anywhere. That no matter where I search, I find only myself.

HOW NICE!

I understand how people equate lovingkindness with Who We Really Are, because that seems to be a natural manifestation of this Empty Awareness. But sometimes it seems so phony. Like we're supposed to be loving all the time. At the group meeting last week everyone was talking so quietly and politely and being so New Agey correct, I wanted to throw up.

Yes, Oneness is not always soft and sweet. Sometimes it's a kick in the groin. Sometimes it's the *Vajra* sword that cuts off your head.

Like when one of the guys started talking about something and you commented by saying it was "bullshit." You could see the teacher right away put his hand out and interrupt like he was afraid we'd break out into a riot. And then everyone was back to talking quietly and nodding and being nice.

I noticed.

Don't you ever want to just jump up and shout?

It's crossed my mind.

Why didn't you, then?

Because it crossed my mind, and moved on.

Like the old Zen Masters, they used to carry a stick and whack their students across the shoulders if they were nodding while meditating. Sometimes I think that's what we need.

Yes.

[Pause] *Are you being nice?*

When? Now?

Yes. Because you don't have much to say on this subject.

Maybe that's because you do.

EMPTINESS

Oddly—or not so oddly—Emptiness can be seen. It is a matter of turning the focus of attention inward, turning it 180 degrees away from "things out there" and resting it here where there is nothing, a nothing large enough and empty enough to accommodate everything—thoughts, feelings, and perceptions—a nothing unlike any other in that it is wide awake, a nothing that is aware capacity for all that comes and goes within it, and—and here's the kicker—a nothing that is aware capacity for all that comes and goes that *is* it. This is Who I Am, and anyone can say the same.

SEEING

You said in an earlier conversation that for all of recorded history the teaching has been conceptual, whereas now it's time for the experiential.

As a friend said, it's been the Word, and now it's the Vision.

So it's the Seeing of God?

Yes, except the Seeing *is* God. There aren't two here. There isn't someone separate, seeing God.

Do you think this Seeing will catch on and become popular?

Probably not in its original form. It's too simple, too direct, too devastating to the ego. Watered down and made into dogma, it might—but then it wouldn't be Seeing, it would be business-as-usual, just another path in a forest of conceptual paths.

But the meaning added on to the Vision is conceptual, no?

Yes, that's true. The Seeing is direct, timeless. The meaning added to it is conceptual, "downstream" of it.

So there is the Vision, followed by the Word. Which is probably the founding principle behind every religion known to man, how every legitimate "way" got started. Someone has the Vision and says, do this and this, and you'll have it too.

Or the way is supplied by others—disciples, followers, or

those in positions of power—often according to whatever meets their personal needs.

So how is Seeing any different? It's the Vision, and like all others, soon it will be turned into the Word.

That could happen. For now, the directive is to *look*, look for yourself and not rely on what others tell you. And by "look," I mean actually *look*. Everything is in the looking.

But I've read that this Seeing is only a pointer, albeit in the right direction, which is "within," but that it is still essentially an experience, and is therefore not the real "awakeness," which is supposedly beyond experience.

I've heard that criticism, and my hunch is that it was proffered by someone who was caught up in the meaning of it—the Word—and who missed the simplicity and availability and ordinariness of Seeing. How often I have heard, "It can't be this easy! It can't be right here!"

So then, is seeing an experience?

Not like other experiences. Not in the sense that one usually attributes to the term. Body-mind experiences *last*, are part and parcel of the thoughts and feelings attached to a separate self. The assumption is that to experience something—an object or an event—the false identity of a separate self must be operative, such that a self (subject) experiences other (objects). But never is this the case. There is only one Experiencer, and that one is Who You Really Are—First-Person Singular, Awake Empty Capacity and all it is capacity for—and although it appears that this one Experiencer experiences objects, in fact there is only the One experiencing the One, Pure Subjectivity experiencing only Itself, God experiencing God, always and ever.

To one who believes he is a separate self, Seeing may seem to be a doorway, but unbeknownst to him, it is also an arrival. Seeing Who You Really Are is not attained to, nor is it Subject to repetition. Every time is the first time. Seeing is not a state of being. It is complete in itself. It is Seeing seeing Seeing, embracing all, holding nothing to Itself but Itself.

So it's the difference between "knowing" and "knowing about"?

Yes, in the sense that it's immediate, unmediated by an ego-self. Knowing is an experience of the Alone by the Alone, and there is the knowledge that every experience, including that which is claimed by an ego-self, is by the Alone.

And here we are, talking about Seeing!

Yes. When one look will do. One look in the right direction.

COMPASSION

Compassion is about the Self, caring for the Self.

Compassion is the urge to give No-thing to Everything.

Compassion is "me" disappearing in favor of "you," knowing I *have* what you look like, and *am* what you are.

Compassion is one "part" (Itself) giving to another "part" (Itself), knowing that there are no parts.

Compassion is pure movement within stillness.

Compassion is play. It is laughter. It is tears.

Compassion is the shedding of a lie, the lifting of a veil, an opening in the clouds to reveal a crystalline sky, and the knowledge that the lie, the veil, and the clouds were all along an expression of compassion.

Compassion is like buying yourself a present, and the whole world is yourself, including the present.

Compassion is an offering to God, every second.

Compassion is said to be like treating your neighbor as you would treat yourself. It isn't. Compassion is knowing that your neighbor *is* yourself.

Compassion is the movement of Pure Subjectivity. Its other names are God, Buddha, Brahma, The Beloved, Self, Tao,

Who You Really Are, Being, and Presence—and none of these are what it is.

KARMA

The last time we talked you said that karma was a "story."

I did? I wonder why.

Have you changed your mind, then?

No, but let's see where it leads.

The idea that what I put out I get back seems perfectly true to me, and it's called karma. What goes around comes around. You yourself said that the world is a mirror image of our thinking.

I did, and that's the case insofar as we believe we're functioning as separate selves in a world of separate things. In the dream of duality, karma rules. As you said, what goes around, even though it might take a while and appear in different forms, inevitably comes around. The balance is always maintained.

So you're saying that from the point of view of the relative, it's real.

It seems real.

And from the point of view of the Absolute?

It's neither real nor unreal.

Even this is a sort of duality—Absolute, and relative.

Only when seen from the point of view of the relative. In fact, there is no duality; there is only the illusion of duality. You are the Absolute, manifesting as a separate self. And since the world is a mirror image of that expression, it too appears as separate and filled with separate things. So there is an apparent you ("self") living in an apparent world ("other"), where cause and effect appear to function. But if you'll simply *look*, you'll see that you're not in the world, the world is in you! With this one look, the spell is broken. You are the Alone, and all of this fabulous ever-changing world, moment by moment, scene by scene, appears and disappears within your embrace.

Is this why it is said that, after enlightenment, a person no longer creates karma?

Yes. A person sees that what they are is not simply a person, but the All. And to the All, cause and effect are not different.

So if I stop trying to be the doer who makes things happen, the world will reflect that?

Yes, to a point. When the ego games stop, when the judgements and expectations no longer operate, the world will present a lighter, more natural face—and it will be your face. But who is the doer who stops being the doer? The point is not to slow and eventually stop the wheel of samsara, but to see it for what it is. Let me ask you, have you ever tried to stop doing anything?

Well, during meditation, I've stopped for a while.

And what was that like? Did the thoughts stop?

No.

Did *anything* stop?

Well, no. Actually, everything continued.

The body continued doing its body thing, everything in the room continued being and doing what it is and does, the world continued being a world. All without your input. All without asking you!

I get the point—it happens without me.

That's because who you think you are, a self, an ego, is not in charge. How huge a joke is it when you think you're making things happen and you find out you're not? Often you hear the meditation instruction to just watch—watch the breath, watch thoughts come and go, watch sights and sounds. The purpose of that is to realize that you have no control over anything and that there is no separate self to exercise such. The true Watcher is "empty," completely impersonal, appearing as all that is watched.

And with that realization, karma stops?

With that realization, it is seen that nothing is actually happening, and therefore that there is no such thing as karma. It is the Absolute, manifesting. And you are the Absolute. Since you are everything there is, where in that Oneness is there a place for karma?

At this point, at the point of no-self, then, does samsara still exist?

Good question! And the answer is a resounding "No." At the point of no-self, the unreal is seen to be real—the only reality there is. Mountains and rivers once again become mountains and rivers—as What You Are! It all "is-es" itself, including the body and mind, which is also itself. And no one at all is doing it. "Itself" is what you are. You can't be anything else because you're all of it.

One just watches, then?

There is watching, accepting, yes. When one thinks they are "one," however, judgements and expectations arise, and it's the judgements and expectations, the wanting of things or events to be different than what they are, that brings suffering. Put that energy out into the world, it comes back as pain, and "one" is caught in the samsaric cycle of cause and effect. Samsara *is* cause and effect. However, when there is no "one," oneSelf is seen to be everything that is, just as it appears, and judgements and expectations have nothing to hold on to. See what you are, and the watching and accepting are automatic.

And attachments? We don't need to get rid of attachments?

No. They'll lose power as a result of seeing what you are. Trying to get rid of attachments can only strengthen them. Having seen what you are, it becomes obvious that the idea of No-thing being attached to No-thing, Everything being attached to Everything, Itself being attached to Itself, is ludicrous. Nothing is needed because it's all what you are. This business of working with karma and attachments is the idea that you can get to nirvana by wearing out the shoe of samsara. For some, dealing with karma and attachments and questioning the validity of the separate self is perhaps a way to undermine the solidity of such beliefs and leave an opening for Awakeness to shine through. But ultimately there's no need to get rid of karma or attachments or even the self, as if one could. Let them take care of themselves. Let it all just be, because it will all just be what it is anyway.

SPACED OUT

Space is no thing. It is not an object. It is not made of parts. Space cannot be separate from anything because all things are made of space. Space cannot be confined because whatever confines it takes up space, and space cannot be open because there is nowhere outside of space for it to be. Space and Awareness are the same, in that space is an aspect of the functioning of Awareness, i.e., Awareness manifesting in what we call "dimensions," though in fact all dimensions are experienced "here."

The same for time. Time is Awareness manifesting as presence, which we feel as "now," and presence is Awareness manifesting as Being, which we feel as "here." Time is Awareness expressing itself via the concept of duration, a result of what appears to be a succession of "nows," giving rise to thoughts of a "past" and a "future," even though such concepts are always experienced "now."

Awareness does not occur in space-time; space-time is the mechanism by which Awareness manifests as the world. Space-time *is* Awareness, functioning as this-and-that, here-and-there, now-and-then. It is Who You Are, spaced out as the universe.

THE ONE BODY

You've said that the definition of enlightenment is that there is no one to be enlightened. But you've also said that What You Are is both No-thing and Everything, and the seeing of that can be called enlightenment. So when the Buddha is enlightened, all beings are enlightened. Do you see what I'm getting at?

Yes, I do. That's a good point, and not an easy one to explain.

So if enlightenment happens, all my levels of appearance, quarks to galaxies, are enlightened, including my human *level.*

Yes.

In that sense, then, I as a human being could be enlightened.

In that sense, yes.

Wow! That's the somersault, isn't it! The front *flip!*

It's coming back for everything, including yourself. It's picking up all the pieces, making it right. It's the bodhisattva's return for others, when there are no "others."

It's once again seeing "mountains and rivers."

Yes, as Who You Are. It's embodiment as The One Body of Christ—all that is, ever was, and ever shall be, right now.

I think you once said that anyone who called themselves enlightened was probably full of beans. You could have been wrong about that, then?

I could have been wrong.

STILLPOINT

Being the One Consciousness, being the pointless point into which everything fits and as which everything is, being No-thing manifesting as all of space and time, I am eternally still.

Here, there is only Pure Consciousness without objects, and therefore nothing to move. Objects and movement appear *in* Consciousness (as Consciousness, moving), and therefore the world of things and events is Stillness Itself, appearing to move.

Take a walk and check to see if you—the One Consciousness—move. Do you move through the scene or does the scene move through you? If you are no-thing, how could you move? If you are everything—that is, if there is nothing and nowhere you are not—how could you move?

Movement happens in the world "out there;" it *is* the world "out there," in that there would be no world without movement. It is what you are—the One Consciousness—manifesting as everything that moves, and all of it happens not "out there" but right here, where there is no movement.

Take a walk and watch your legs stride, the sidewalk approach and disappear into your Emptiness, the buildings and trees jostle and change shape and pass by. Or rather, take the world for a walk, while you watch from this still and pointless point. It's all Who You Are, the One Consciousness, Stillness Itself, on the move.

STORIES

Lately I've been doing two-way looking—consciously looking back at what is looking while at the same time looking out at the scene—and I think I noticed what you were talking about before when you said that things take on a vividness, a beauty. Colors become enhanced, sounds are richer, even stuff in the trash seems more special, if you know what I mean.

I do.

And it doesn't matter what it is, although flowers are really beautiful when seen this way. I mean, it can be a pencil or a candy-wrapper, just as easily as a sunset. Nor do I think about the improbability of there being anything at all, and the astonishment of that. It's just relaxing into what's happening, you know? But here's my question: Science says that there is no sound and no color in nature, that these qualities are in the eyes and ears of the beholder—frequencies of light waves and compression waves interpreted as color and sound. So although I see I am replaced by that flower and am pure capacity for that music, science says, No, those are sights and sounds in your head.

Yes, that's third-person thinking. Science is the study and manipulation of "things," of objects in the world, and it is extremely successful in that endeavor—the discoveries and innovations are too numerous to mention. But science can never explain First-Person-Singular, which is not a thing. Like religion, it can show us a way, even lead us to the door, but it can never open it.

And sometimes, science trips over itself, especially in the realms of nearest and farthest, smallest and largest. It doesn't do well with nothing or everything. These areas aren't usually the domain of science anyway, and of course the greater part of science today is in commercial application.

So we spin these stories about how things work, and sometimes the story backfires. Take, for instance, science's story of how you see. Light from the sun in the form of wave-particles strikes an object—say, that cup—and while some of the light is absorbed, the rest is reflected outward, a portion of which enters the lens and forms an upside-down image at the back of your eye, causing changes in the light-sensitive cells there. This results in changes to the chemical in which those cells are embedded, which in turn causes electro-chemical impulses to be passed along the optic nerve to a particular area of the brain where these messages are "processed," presumably the processing being carried out by the molecules, atoms, and particles of brain cells—and somehow somewhere within the quantum reality of this mysterious terminus there is reproduced the image of a cup.

However, what is strange about this story is that, in proving that the cup exists as an image in your head, it disproves the fact of it existing "out there"—or of anything at all existing out there—a result that science surely can't have intended. For all you know, what happens at the quantum level in your head may in no way resemble what exists in the world, if in fact there *is* a world.

Second, if the story is true and there really is no world, what about your head? Are not the brain cells that do the processing a part of the world? Are they somehow exempt?

Third, how is it that the image of a cup actually forms in your head? Are there cells, molecules, atoms in the shape of a cup lurking somewhere, waiting to be called? And how does something the size of a car manage to fit there? Could the image appear holographically? Perhaps. But this brings me to the last point:

No matter how the image appears, how is it that you actually experience it?

Yes, this last point is crucial, isn't it? Because the story doesn't tell me how I actually experience anything.

The story is one of objects connecting with objects. Science takes for granted the existence of a you-object here and a world-object there, so then the problem arises of how one apparently connects with the other. The result is the above story. And as I mentioned, science is very successful in the study and manipulation of objects. But it fails to explain Subjectivity, and for a very good reason: Science itself, the method, the very language of science, is objective.

So how do I really see anything?

Ah—I thought you'd never ask!

Let me guess—it's the First-Person-Singular story.

Yes. And to First-Person-Singular, it's *all* a story, including this one. But let me tell it anyway because it's so much easier to swallow, and it's closer to the truth—that is, it points in the right direction.

The First-Person-Singular story is that you are both the Center of the universe and the universe as a Whole. You are Awake No-thing and the All that appears within It. How do you see anything? You *are* it. Here at the Center there is no eye, no brain, nothing to receive signals or thoughts about those signals, nothing in the way—in fact, nothing at all this side of that cup, or the desk, or that car, or the mountains. Here, there is only pure experience, pure Aware Capacity and all it is capacity for. This is how you see. Eyes don't see. Only What You Are sees, and sees only Itself. This is true of hearing, smelling, tasting, and touching. Sense experience doesn't happen to a "thing" in the world, it happens to Aware Emptiness *as* the world.

So the First-Person-Singular story says, you don't live in the world, it lives in you as What You Are, and it does so *exactly as it appears*, in all its riotous beauty, immediate and unmediated. No wonder colors are brighter and sounds are richer. No wonder the flower is gorgeous and the candy-wrapper shines. It's all You, and nowhere else but Here where you are.

You said that this story is easier to swallow, but not so for a mind conditioned to believe otherwise. But I'll say this—the First-person-Singular story leaves me with a smile on my heart, and I say "heart" because right now I'm not sure I have a face!

Good! Certain stories have their value, after all.

FRONT FLIP

The world is not in the eye of the beholder. There is no beholder other than the world itself. Such qualities as color and shape, sound and taste, odor and texture, beauty and ugliness, are attached to the objects they describe, not imprisoned as individual (and private) experiences in the heads of presumed beholders. The world is not, as science would have us believe, the "inane play of inscrutable energies," but fully alive and kicking, noisily displaying itself moment by moment in a kaleidoscope of form beyond its own wildest imagination.

Things aren't as they seem, they are as they *are*. That object called a "tree" is no less a tree because of the thought "tree" attached to it. There is no separate thinker to call it a "tree." It really is a tree, exactly as it is, exactly as it's called. Fundamentally, it is the tree observing and calling itself "tree," and it is What I Am, "tree-ing."

The same is true of a body-mind. A body-mind is no less a body-mind because of the thought "body-mind" attached to it. A body-mind is not simply a belief or a bundle of sensations and therefore an illusion. It really is a body-mind, and it is What I Am, "body-mind-ing."

So it is for "you" and "me." You are no less "you" and I am no less "me" because of the thoughts attached to our objective manifestations. You are really "you" and I am really "me," and What I Am is Room for you and me and everything, and I find it all inside of What I Am, exactly as it is. "You" and "me" are What I Am, "you-ing" and "me-ing."

The world is filled with meaning and purpose not because of a mistaken view. The world is filled with meaning and purpose because it is What I Am, and I find Myself filled with meaning and purpose, all the meaningful and purposeful thoughts attached to the world moment by moment that lend it life and beauty and love, and these thoughts *are* the world, exactly as it is, and it is What I Am, "worlding," bursting with life and beauty and love.

There are no mistakes. It is as it is. I Am That I Am.

HIDE-AND-SEEK

How much of what you're saying is actually true?

None of it is true.

Then why do we have these talks?

I don't know. Apparently What You Really Are—Pure Subjectivity—wants to coax you out of your identity as a personal self.

But what exactly is happening? If none of what you're saying is true, then what is?

Absolutely nothing is happening, and nothing said is true. Truth cannot be told. It can be seen, it can be intuited, but it can't be described in words because words are conceptual representations of that which manifests as objective reality, while Truth is Pure Subjectivity, and Pure Subjectivity cannot be described.

I don't understand what you mean when you say, "Nothing is happening." To me, things are happening all the time.

What you think is happening is your *story* of what is happening, based on mental imagery which you call the "past," and expectations which you call the "future." But past and future are conceptual constructs via which Pure Subjectivity manifest Itself, and there is only Pure Subjectivity. Pure Subjectivity is the only reality, manifesting as a world in which a "you" and a zillion other objects appear to exist separately and interact with each other.

So you're saying that I produce space and time and everything in it?

No. As who you think you are, you don't do anything. This "you" you refer to arises with space and time, and as such, is an appearance.

Then who does it?

No one. It is What You Really Are, Pure Subjectivity prior to the story of "you" and "me."

I really can't see that. The term "Pure Subjectivity" has no meaning for me.

Because it's an objective representation of that which can never be objective. All I can say is to look within, knowing that there is no separate "you" who can decide to do so. It's actually very strange, this asking you to look within, because there aren't two of us here, or even one. Pure Subjectivity is asking Pure Subjectivity to look at Itself? It's as if Pure Subjectivity plays this game of hide-and-seek, disguises Itself as a "you" and then comes along and tells Itself to look at Itself so it can find Itself!

Well, frankly, when it comes to Pure Subjectivity, I'm just completely lost.

My point exactly!

NOT AN ILLUSION

"Those who tell you that our everyday world, the world we see from the perspective of Yesh [being], is illusory and without consequence are wrong. This everyday world is of supreme value, for it—no less than Ayin [emptiness]—is of God."

Rabbi Rami Shapiro, in *Open Secrets*

Once again, the world of things is not an illusion. The illusion is in thinking it is separate from Who You Really Are, from Emptiness, from Aware No-thing. For You are No-thing filled with Everything, Aware Capacity and what it is capacity for, Consciousness and its contents. They are two sides of the same coin, so that the everyday world of things and events is Who You Are, manifesting as things and events. This is why the everyday world is of supreme value and of great consequence—it is You, appearing as this and that, appearing as now and then, appearing as every thought, every feeling, every event, every thing, all space and time, the universe itself. Seeing Who You Are is seeing the priceless and astounding perfection of God, and God is Love, seeing only Itself.

ALL FOR ONE AND ONE FOR ALL

I read that everything is consciousness, but how can I tell? Things don't look conscious. That table, for instance, isn't conscious.

Right. There are no separate consciousnesses. Consciousness is only here. But so is everything else. "Here" is where all is experienced, where Experience itself is.

There is only one consciousness, then.

There is only consciousness, without the "one." I call it First-Person-Singular, Present Tense, as well as many other names. It's only here. In fact, there is no "there."

Then that table is consciousness.

Right. It's not conscious, it doesn't sport a separate table-consciousness; rather, it *is* consciousness, appearing as a table.

The same consciousness I see when I look back at what is looking?

The same wide-open, empty, boundless consciousness filled with the scene. It's what you are.

Yes, but how do I know that that table is what I am?

Well, for one thing, you see it inside of you, inside of the consciousness that you are. Everything is inside of What

You Are, and therefore *is* you.

I see that it's inside of consciousness, but it's still over there, and I don't experience it as "here" like I do myself.

Then let's put it this way: Whatever you go all the way up to, you lose, and find only yourself—consciousness. The table is a manifestation of What You Really Are, and you can prove it scientifically by going all the way up to it.

For instance, taking exactly what you see and not what you've been told or assume—in other words, going on present evidence, which is the scientific method—you the observer approach the table to find out what it is made of, and therefore what it is. Closing in, you lose it as a "table" and observe only a part—say, the top—and closer still you lose it as a table part and discover layers of shellac and wood stain, then the grain of the wood itself. With instruments, you approach even closer, and losing it as wood, you discover the cellular, molecular, and atomic layers, then the mysterious realm of particles, quarks, and fleeting wisps of energy in vast empty space where there is no longer an objective world. And yet there still remains a very present something, and that something, although it is no "thing," is you, the observer. Whatever you go all the way up to, you lose as an appearance and discover only yourself, exactly what that object was an appearance of to begin with. And by "yourself," I mean consciousness, What You Really Are.

I could do that with you also.

Yes! And discover...

That I am you. That you are an appearance of What I Am.

Exactly.

It's why consciousness is called "source," right? Because that's all there is, when you get down to it.

Yes, when you get down to it—all the way down.

What I'm looking out of is what everyone else, every animal, every insect, is looking out of. What I'm looking out of is what everything is! Whew!... This is mind-blowing!

Yes, it blows the mind right off its throne. What You Are was never mind. A famous Ch'an Master once said, "Never mind the mind." Mind, or all the thoughts and beliefs whirl-pooling around the original thought (the "original sin"?) of "I am this individual, this body and mind, this separate person", is just another manifestation of consciousness, of What You Really Are. Actually, it's how the world appears.

And consciousness—What I Really Am—is at the center of it.

Both the center and the periphery. What You Really Are is all of it, No-thing and Everything.

Good Lord!... I've seen this before, and it's almost overwhelming.

Well, you can see it anytime, simply by looking back where you thought you had a face: No-thing filled with Everything, consciousness and what it is conscious of. And although it may seem overwhelming at the moment, it's really quite ordinary. It's the natural way of seeing and being, which, by the way, are one and the same.

Seeing being Being, and Being being Seeing.

Yes, if you want to put it that way.

I like that—"Seeing being Being, and Being being Seeing."

Yes, since you see what it means. But go around saying that to everyone, they'll lock you in the dungeon.

Hee hee! Yeah, saying that, and pointing back at where I don't see a face!

Right. And where they *do*. But of course, anyone can say it. Anyone can see for themselves What They Really Are, and if they do, they'll laugh with you, *as* you.

And if they don't?

Well, then, in the best of times, those so-called "others" will scratch their heads. In the worst of times, you might want to prepare yourself for crucifixion.

HISTORY

It seems to happen like this: God tells stories and seems to forget that He is telling them about Himself. He pretends He's an "other" up against other "others," thereby creating something called a "world" that appears to consist of separate parts based on the opposites of this and that, up and down, here and there, now and then, me and not-me. And as if this weren't amazing enough, for no apparent reason He seems to dawn on Himself that this isn't the way He really is, and then he abides as what He always was, no matter what He otherwise pretended to be but never was to begin with! It was all God's story, is now and ever shall be, told by the Great His-story-ian Himself.

Of course, the above is just a story. But when you come down to it, who is there other than God to tell it?

BLASPHEMY

You know, some people, if they haven't said so already, will call your message blasphemy.

I didn't know I had a message, but since you think I do, how is it blasphemous?

Like when you call yourself God. When you identify with the Absolute. You don't think that's blasphemy?

On the contrary, it's those who set themselves up as separate selves who commit blasphemy. Claiming authorship of their so-called lives—and too often the lives of others—they are the ones who say, "Not Thy will be done, Lord, but mine."

That's a strong statement. There are a lot of good people out there who do good things.

No doubt. But even good people cause suffering. Believing that one determines one's life, invariably there are expectations and disappointments, and the best one can hope for is a story.

A story? What about Bill Gates, who gives billions to charity? What about Einstein or Mozart or Michelangelo? You call their lives mere stories?

All lives are stories. They're God's dream. I can't speak for Gates or the others, but anyone who holds the belief that they exist apart from God, is missing the majesty of What

Is, and What Is is No-thing filled with Everything, generous beyond compare, creative beyond belief.

So you're basically lumping together notables such as Einstein and Mozart with the Hitlers and Stalins of this world, saying there's no difference in their lives?

Relatively, to those of us who believe we're a "someone" engaged in an important event called a "life," there's a huge difference. Hitler and Stalin and the millions of criminals before and since are an example of the concept of self-determination taken to the extreme—it's the "I'm in charge, I know best, I'm getting mine" mentality that's so prevalent today, a case of misplaced identity played out to the limit. But when the identity with a separate self drops away, what remains is God—and whether you were called Bill Gates or Adolf Hitler matters no more and no less than anything else in appearance. The question is, Who are you? Believing you are a separate, self-existing individual who is in charge of his so-called life and who can influence his surroundings to his or anyone else's benefit, is the story of the archangel Lucifer, usurping the role of God. There's the real blasphemy!

And you're God?

Me? Good heavens, no. What you see here is a character in a play written and produced by God, A.K.A. The Absolute, Presence, Tao, Unborn Awareness, Self, Buddhamind, Brahma, The Beloved, and all the other attempts to name the unnameable. Pick one, or juggle them all so none grows stale with use—no matter what you call THIS, it's the only reality. And I am That. But why are you smiling?

Partly because your enthusiasm is contagious, but mostly because I was thinking how much easier it is just to call you a blasphemer.

Yes, I suppose it can seem easier to miss the point, but the truth is, once you see What You Really Are, you also see how difficult it is to build and maintain the deception of the false self. Blasphemy is hard work, and to get the heat off you, you need to call others blasphemers, never realizing that in that very act you are calling yourself one.

Wow! We went from me calling you a blasphemer to you calling me one!

Pretty slick, don't you think?

I guess!

THE LAST DUALITY

I know no other consciousness. There is only *this* consciousness, only here, only now. It is the only one I see, the only one experienced as "I." To assume that you have a separate consciousness apart from this consciousness would be disingenuous at best. It would be the same as saying that a photo or the image in a mirror has its own separate consciousness. There is only one consciousness, and it is big enough, roomy enough, for everyone and everything.

To check this, cut the bottom off a paper bag, find a friend and have them place their face in one end while you look in the other end. Taking for evidence exactly what you see, not what you assume, notice that all the matter appears at that end, and all the consciousness at this end. To assume that there is consciousness at that end or matter at this end is the double lie of duality; it is to "miss the mark," to live in "sin," and the cause of much of the suffering in this world.

For some, this separation of consciousness and matter is a necessary step in the direction of awakening, perhaps the last door to the "House of the Lord." Necessary in order to break the fixation with "things" and allow the seeing of emptiness. Necessary because pure consciousness is empty, void, while the world of things is full, form, and seeing these as two is a prelude to seeing the One: Emptiness/Fullness, Void/Form as one. Both are the same, together they are God, and there is nothing that is not God.

SOMETHING LOST, SOMETHING GAINED

How am I replaced by the scene? I don't get it.

Let's do something silly and childish. And like the other awareness exercises we did, go only on present evidence, only what you see, hear, or feel in the moment, without relying on what you've learned from others or assume to be true.

Okay.

Sit on this stool and face the window. Now close your eyes, and I'm going to stand behind you. We've done this first part before, so you'll be familiar with it. Answer the following questions to yourself or to me if you want: How tall or how wide are you? How many toes do you have? How many legs, if any? Arms? Where do you end and where does the world begin? What do you really look like to others?

Yes, on present evidence it's impossible to say. I could be a mile wide or the size and shape of a worm. Being truthful in this situation is very strange.

Okay, now I'm going to reach around you and take your hands—that is, what *I* see as hands, from over here—and place them, like this, on what *I* see as your ears, and ask you to hold them. So—are you holding your ears?

Not from my point of view. Here, there are only sensations. I can't truthfully say whether or not there are hands or ears involved.

Right. And between those sensations, how much space is there?

I don't know. It could be no space at all, it could be a mile, or it could be infinite.

Now open your eyes—that is, what *I* see as eyes—and tell me what you see between those sensations.

Yes, it's the scene!

What would you say is the distance between the sensations?

Still, it's infinite. The scene, and nothing else, is between them.

So you're the scene.

It's more like I'm wearing the scene, and that includes this upside-down body from the chest down. Or, I mean, up.

What else?

The window, the mountains and sky.

What about your head?

There's no head. There's just the scene, and these sensations.

So you could say that your face is the scene.

Yeah. That's a trip!

Now turn around and look this way, and tell me what you have for a face.

Your face.

As I have yours. So... who you thought you were...

Is replaced with the scene! Yes, no doubt, no doubt. Without the learned beliefs of what I look like to others, I'm the scene, just as it is.

You lost a head and gained the world. Amazing what a little silliness can do, no?

THE PORTAL

As Primordial Awareness, all that I see, hear, taste, touch, and smell is what I am, manifesting, and all that I manifest as, is, in that sense, a mirror, a reflection of what I am. A bird, the sound of a passing truck, hot tea, a lingering fragrance—each is what-I-am-in-manifestation, and therefore each has the ability to "remind" me of what I am.

And there is one manifestation that, because it is so "close to home," so familiar (after all, for most of my life I believed it was who I *was*), and because it is so different from others of its kind, is the ultimate of all reminders. It is this body, seen from here.

Unlike other bodies over there, this body is the key to discovering what I really am, if only I take notice. And notice I do, for, given the present evidence, how much more obvious could it be? Those bodies are headed, are right-side-up, are similar in general shape and proportions, and come in various sizes depending on their perceived "distance" from where I am. This body, however, is upside-down, with little feet on top, truncated legs and a wide trunk with enormous shoulders below, and at the very bottom, this Boundless Awake Capacity, an emptiness so clear and so vast that everything above easily fits within it.

Eating or drinking, those bodies place morsels of food or pour various liquids into fleshy slits in their faces, while here each morsel of food and sip of liquid disappears into this Boundless Capacity, and taste appears, the sensations of texture and temperature, of "chewing" and "swallowing" appear, all of it accompanied by various aromas. No such experience occurs when others eat, but here in this awake emptiness, the amazing happens, and routinely at that! Others

116

move through the scene, walking, running, or passing by in cars, but here nothing moves; rather, it is the scene that moves through me, within me.

Others fall asleep for hours every night, but here nothing of the sort happens. This upside-down body lies prone on the bunk, various scenes come and go, some of them bizarre indeed, and then this upside-down body climbs off the bunk, and I notice that the clock reads seven hours ahead.

These are some of the ways that *this* body, the First-Person body, is the ultimate reminder of what I really am, which is Boundless Awake Capacity, AKA Primordial Awareness. It is this First-Person body, so familiar and so different from those other second and third-person bodies, that is the portal, both the key and the gate to the true ground, the foundation of all that can be said to "be."

Have a look. Your body is pointing out the obvious. After all, what is your body but what you really are—Primordial Awareness—manifesting itself? And why shouldn't it point to itself in this most extraordinary and yet ordinary way?

NEVERMIND THE MIND

Some people say you've lost your mind.

Really! I didn't think they had noticed.

So you admit it?

Of course. Whatever mind there is, I certainly can't claim it.

How can you say that? Everyone has a mind.

Mind appears as part of the world, and is attached to the things of the world. It is thoughts and feelings that are part and parcel of what they are thoughts and feelings about. The things of this world—the world itself—cannot be separated from the thoughts that adhere to them, the thoughts that comprise them. Mind is nothing more than this. What I Am is No-thing, Pure Awareness, and mind comes and goes in that.

How, then, do you explain the different memories we all have? Don't tell me they aren't personal to each individual!

They *are* personal, in that they are attached to "individuals," which are also "things" in the world. But all of this is an expression of Pure Awareness. It is Pure Awareness appearing as "memories had by individuals," but never being other than Pure Awareness, and in that, they are all alike. There is actually no difference between "your" memories and "my" memories, any more than there is a difference between "your" view of the room as you are standing facing me and "my" view in the opposite direction, although the content may appear to be different. All are reflections of the One who is No-thing. They appear to be different because this is the mechanism whereby the world appears. This is all part of the great game of "self" and "other." Which, by the way, taken to the limit, can point to the absence of "self" and "other."

How so?

Because ultimate subject is No-thing and ultimate object is Everything, and they are not different. What I am is Aware Capacity filled with everything it is capacity for, and this has been termed Pure Subjectivity.

And profoundly seeing this is what is called "awakening"?

Yes, but this too can be misleading because it implies that there is someone who is asleep. There is only Awakeness, already awake. From the point of view of a seeker, awakening is sought, but this is like a character in a dream striving to wake up, when in fact they are being dreamed.

But from the point of view of a seeker, awakening is hugely important, the only thing that really matters.

Yes, and that only serves to keep the belief of being a separate self intact.

But I've heard you say that everything matters.

Yes, from the point of view of Clarity, everything matters, including the belief in a separate self, because it is Pure Awareness expressing itself as "separate self."

So from the point of view of Clarity, does everything change for the better, and become more meaningful?

No, and yes. Nothing changes, but all is seen anew. Trying to get something is replaced by gratitude for being it.

This is confusing. I've read that awakening is extremely rare, and now I know why.

It only seems that way because you think you're separate.

Okay—say there are seven billion humans on the planet and several billion more animals, not to mention insects and plants which at least have some rudimentary form of awareness—all these beings, and maybe only a handful of them are truly awake. Would you deny that?

All there is, is Awareness.

What?

There are not billions or trillions of awarenesses. There is only Awareness.

How can that be?

Who knows? But you can see it for yourself. Look back. Direct your attention 180 degrees from where you normally look, and look at what you are looking out of. Awareness "sees" itself thus as nothing, void, empty—and fully aware. Now tell me, do you see another awareness anywhere else in the room?

No.

Have you *ever* seen another awareness?

No, I guess not.

That's because there *isn't* another awareness. There is only Awareness, and it is void, empty, and always here. It is Presence, and therefore never absent. It is what you are and all that you are, and if you'll notice, the whole world—every object, thought, feeling, event—everything fits within its scope. It is No-thing/Everything.

Yes. But this means…

That you are alone? Yes, and what's more, you are *the* Alone.

Wait a minute. This is…

Yes?

I've been in this spot before with you. We started off talking about your having lost your mind, and now it's like I'm losing mine.

Yes.

Could we take a break?

Of course.

A WIN-WIN SITUATION

What I see when I look here is No-thing, awake to the world, awake to itself. This No-thing is obviously Who I Am. As No-thing, I am free because, what is there to be bound? For that matter, what is there to be free? No-thing is so free it is free of the concept of freedom.

What I see when I look here is Everything—that is, everything that appears within this No-thing. This Everything is also obviously Who I Am. But all that appears—the entire passing show—is just that: passing! I am free of whatever appears because it disappears, moment by moment.

As No-thing I am free because there is nothing to be bound. As Everything I am free because there is nothing outside of everything to bind me. It's a win-win situation, whenever I look. Even whenever I don't look.

THE POINT IS MOOT

So you're saying that there's no choice whatsoever, that everything just shows up of its own accord?

From the point of view of the separate self—the so-called "mistaken view" —no, there is no choice.

By saying "so-called," do you mean that the body-mind isn't a mistaken view?

There are no mistakes. Believing that one is located in a body and mind, or *is* a body and mind, is exactly as it should be, simply because it is. It's all God, functioning, even when disguised as self and other.

So there's a body-mind, and an ego-self attached to that, and it's not an illusion?

No, it's not an illusion. Not when you know it's Who You Are, appearing as that.

But when you don't know?

Then it's *called* an illusion, and issuing from that, the idea of a "real" separate self choosing this or that is also an illusion. The premise is false, so all that follows is false. However, as I said, it's all God, it's all Who You Really Are, and so, in reality, the One Chooser—Who You Really Are—chooses everything you consciously want, everything you unconsciously want, and everything that shows up anyway. What you are is the whole ball of wax, and it's chosen by the whole ball of wax.

So you're saying that Who I Am chooses to be separate, chooses to be housed in a body-mind and call itself a separate self?

Exactly. Awareness chooses from an infinity of possibilities, all of which are Itself. It's so free it can even choose to be bound.

Yes, but the belief that I have free will as an individual is so strong, I can't imagine that there isn't some basis of truth behind it.

Well, you're right. The basis of truth is that Who You Really Are, A.K.A. No-thing/Everything, is Free Will Itself, is the One Chooser of all that is, and this is what you feel.

It chooses even Itself.

Yes! That's the miracle! All of it chooses all of it. Itself chooses Itself.

You hear a lot about "no doer," "no choice," and that just doesn't feel right to me. Like when you said there was "no choice" at the Buddhist meeting and everyone reacted negatively, maybe you were wrong.

Yes, you have a point—and it *is* depressing, isn't it, hearing *ad nauseum* that there is no doer, no choice? It's also fundamentally untrue, as we've said. I said what I said because everyone was locked into the sense of being separate selves and having free will from that perspective, but harping on "no doer," "no choice" is a good way to reify that very sense of separate self, no?

It seems that way.

The essential understanding is, as Who We Really Are, we have complete freedom. Even the freedom to identify with an appearance and call it a separate self, even the freedom to forget that we've done this, moment by moment, and thus believe and feel this to be factually true: "I am this body-mind and I can exercise free will, can choose to do this or that."

In reality, however, we have no freedom from this point of view because the point of view is *not* factually true—all along it was Who We Really Are, *pretending* to be who we really aren't! And knowing this, there is no longer any need to harp on the absence of doership. The question of choice is answered, and both the question and the answer come from the same source: Who We Really Are.

A further way to look at it is this: As No-thing, there is no one and nothing to be free or bound, to choose or not choose. As Everything, there is nothing separate from the whole to be free or bound, to choose or not choose. In either case, the point is moot.

I CALL MYSELF "I"

I call myself "I" because there is this undeniable sense of presence, of *being*. And where does it come from? It comes from nowhere, from nothing. It comes from, it comes for, it *is* for no reason at all, except perhaps to say exactly what is said here by itself about itself. Who am I? How do I get to *be?*, it asks, knowing of course that it is asking itself, that the puzzle of Who I Am is Who I Am asking Who I Am.

I am both the seer and the seen. I am the seen seeing itself. I am the witness witnessing that which is witnessed, and that which is witnessed is the witness witnessing. I might say that the world is a mirror of What I Am, but this isn't quite true. The world *is* What I Am.

Perhaps this makes little sense, and yet it gushes forth as joy for your sake, for my sake, for heaven's sake.

"To be saved is to be Him." And He is "I," this Eye, into which everything appears and disappears as Him, as "I," as Who I Am.

SOURCE

How is Awareness the source *of the universe? Why call it the source of anything?*

One answer is that Awareness can exist without the universe, but the universe cannot exist without Awareness. It is said that, even if there is nothing to be aware of, Awareness is aware, and proof of this is found in deep sleep when there are no objects, when only Awareness is present. However, this to me is an assumption. It is not my experience that I fall into a state called "deep sleep" in which there is Pure Awareness but no objects to be aware of, dream or otherwise. Only in retrospect is there such a state, an imagined state.

Speaking as First-Person-Singular, Present Tense, I am Aware No-thing filled with whatever appears within it. I see this. For instance, I am Aware No-thing filled with the cell, the bunk, the metal desk, the radio and TV, the clock which reads 10:45 P.M., two legs and a torso stretched out on the bunk, flying bodiless over a tropical beach, three strangers and my grandfather on the back of an elephant, an argument with my cat in the bathtub, unease over money matters in a room that is vaguely familiar, my wife chopping vegetables, the alarm going off, the clock reading 6:00 A.M., legs and torso and arms swinging out of the bunk, pants going on, socks on, feet into shoes, shirt on, the tier passing below, legs striding, the chowhall door approaching, breakfast on the way.

No breaks. Someone else, a third-person party "out there," may say I slept nearly seven hours, and "prove" this by showing me the difference in clock time, but from the perspective of Who I Really Am, there is no break in Awareness, not even for an instant. It all happens here in this uninterrupted awake Space for whatever fills it—including the elasticity of space/time.

What about the gaps between thoughts that some teachers talk about?

Here, there are no gaps. Or, it's all gap. Thoughts, objects, "events" come and go in this Awareness. How could there be gaps in nothing?

And it's this uninterrupted Aware Space that is the source of all that comes and goes?

Yes, and no. This Aware Space here, this No-thing, *never* comes and goes. Anything and everything that appears within it *always* comes and goes. So yes, we call this Awareness the "source" of all that appears within it. However, this is not to imply cause and effect. What God is, is No-thing/Everything, as One. So we can put this in two ways: First, as Everything, all-that-is appears as one, moves as one, is one. Everything is not only interdependent and interconnected to everything else, it *is* everything else, is the Totality, and everything that is done is done by the Totality.

Second, as No-thing, Awareness is *capacity* for the scene—the scene *is* the Totality—appearing spontaneously within it, such that the scene is one with Awareness and Awareness is one with the scene. This is perceived by that very same Awareness/Scene—which is to say that Awareness/Scene is perceiving Itself! Whatever appears is in fact Awareness appearing. The Totality is Awareness manifesting as the Totality, Itself *itselfing.*

Then nothing is really the source.

Yes, Nothing is really the source. And no, nothing is really the source. Take your pick.

SELF-PORTRAIT

I am...

Self-aware, Self-begotten, Self-created, Self-generated, Self-propagating, Self-propelled, Self-motivated, Self-adjusting, Self-controlled, Self-employed, Self-correcting, Self-sufficient, Self-supported, Self-taught, Self-acting, Self-contained, Self-addressed, Self-centered, Self-dependent, Self-evident, Self-existent, Self-fulfilled, Self-delighted.

Self-winding!

OH SHUT UP!

You said in your article that you were in awe of walking through yourself. What did you mean?

Actually, that's a little misleading. Or let's say it's a partial truth. At the time I wrote that, I recognized that I was everything, that I was the scene just the way it appeared, and so I said I was walking through myself. But actually I wasn't going anywhere, never have and never will. What I Am is No-thing, Stillness Itself, and always *the scene moves through Me.* From the First-Person perspective, everything moves within Me, through Me, *as* Me. It's all internal.

So how would you put it now?

Well, I don't know. How about, "What I Am is in awe of What-I-Am-As-Everything moving through What-I-Am-As-No-thing?"

Awkward.

Yes, and way too wordy. How about, "Itself awes Itself itself-ing?"

Nah, the image is lost.

Okay, then let's go back to the original. Aware No-thing is in awe seeing feet and legs striding, the sidewalk and lawn floating by. All of it is What I Am. Pure Awareness as No-thing, and Pure Awareness appearing as feet, sidewalk, and lawn flowing by, and Pure Awareness manifesting as awe. So

... "I am in awe of walking through myself."

Still.... Maybe there's a better way to put it.

Maybe we should just shut up!

INCARNATION

Shall we not celebrate the Incarnation? Is not the Incarnation the revelation that God is the son, void is form, emptiness is fullness, spirit is body? For Christ is born unceasingly as What You Are, awake and filled with the scene. Saint Paul said, "Put ye on the Lord Jesus Christ." You might as well, considering that you already have. His hands are holding this book!

Acknowledgements

Thank you Joe Ayers, who has blessed me with his friendship and support for so many years. Thank you Fr. Bob, without whose encouragement I might never have looked within. Thank you Joan Tollifson for your wonderful books and for your generous review of mine. Thank you Chris S., Charlie B., Brad W., and Paul J., seers and friends on the "outside" looking in. Thank you Barbara for sharing this same Awake Space during your visits. Thank you Catherine Harding for your letters and for your efforts in translating into French the Vision to end all visions. Thank you Richard Lang for seeing and being THIS, and for your tireless enthusiasm in showing so many Who they really are. Thank you Julian Noyce for the fine job with my books, and for publishing so many wonderful others on non-duality. Thank you Michael Adamson, Chris Cheney, Jim Clatfelter, Melanie Gamble, Steve Holloway, Nancye Mercer for typing and editing the manuscript; I so much appreciate your help. Thank you Zachary R. for the reproduction of Douglas Harding's drawings of the First-Person-Singular; I am also indebted to the late Mr. Harding for the awareness exercises and many of the ideas presented in this book. Thanks to Anthony, Andrew, Chris, Bill, John, Jacob, Scott, and all the other members of the Buddhist sangha here, and to Fred and Gary for making the long drive once a month to teach us what in our hearts we already know. And a very special thanks to Jan Hamer—for your letters of friendship and encouragement, for your willingness to celebrate the One with such clarity and honesty, and for all your help in getting this book to print.

CONSCIOUS.TV is a TV channel which broadcasts on the Internet at www.conscious.tv. It also has programmes shown on several satellite and cable channels round the world including the Sky system in the UK where you can watch programmes at 9pm every evening on channel No 275. The channel aims to stimulate debate, question, enquire, inform, enlighten, encourage and inspire people in the areas of Consciousness, Non-Duality and Science. It also has a section called 'Life Stories' with many fascinating interviews.

There are over 200 interviews to watch including several with communicators on Non-Duality including Jeff Foster, Steve Ford, Suzanne Foxton, Gangaji, Greg Goode, Scott Kiloby, Richard Lang, Francis Lucille, Roger Linden, Wayne Liquorman, Jac O'Keefe, Mooji, Catherine Noyce, Tony Parsons, Halina Pytlasinska, Genpo Roshi, Satyananda, Richard Sylvester, Rupert Spira, Florian Schlosser, Mandi Solk, James Swartz, and Pamela Wilson. There is also an interview with UG Krishnamurti. Some of these interviewees also have books available from Non-Duality Press.

Do check out the channel as we are interested in your feedback and any ideas you may have for future programmes. Email us at info@conscious.tv with your ideas or if you would like to be on our email newsletter list.

WWW.CONSCIOUS.TV

CONSCIOUS.TV and NON-DUALITY PRESS
present two unique DVD releases

CONVERSATIONS ON NON-DUALITY – VOLUME 1
Tony Parsons – The Open Secret • Rupert Spira –
The Transparency of Things – Parts 1 & 2 • Richard Lang –
Seeing Who You Really Are

CONVERSATIONS ON NON-DUALITY – VOLUME 2
Jeff Foster – Life Without a Centre • Richard Sylvester –
I Hope You Die Soon • Roger Linden – The Elusive Obvious

Available to order from: www.non-dualitypress.com

New Book now available to order from Non-Duality Press

Conversations on Non-Duality
Twenty-Six Awakenings

The book explores the nature of true happiness, awakening, enlightenment and the 'Self' to be realised. It features 26 expressions of liberation, each shaped by different life experiences and offering a unique perspective.

The collection explores the different ways 'liberation' happened and 'suffering' ended. Some started with therapy, self-help workshops or read books written by spiritual masters, while others travelled to exotic places and studied with gurus. Others leapt from the despair of addiction to drugs and alcohol to simply waking up unexpectedly to a new reality.

The 26 interviews included in the book are with: David Bingham, Daniel Brown, Sundance Burke, Katie Davis, Peter Fenner, Steve Ford, Jeff Foster, Suzanne Foxton, Gagaji, Richard Lang, Roger Linden, Wayne Liquorman, Francis Lucille, Mooji, Catherine Noyce, Jac O'Keeffe, Tony Parsons, Bernie Prior, Halina Pytlasinska, Genpo Roshi, Florian Schlosser, Mandi Solk, Rupert Spira, James Swartz, Richard Sylvester and Pamela Wilson.

CPSIA information can be obtained
at www.ICGtesting.com
Printed in the USA
FSOW02n0852091016
25930FS